STANDING
STRONG

MACARTHUR STUDY SERIES

STANDING STRONG

How To Resist the
Enemy of Your Soul

JOHN MACARTHUR

David C Cook®
transforming lives together

STANDING STRONG
Published by David C. Cook
4050 Lee Vance View
Colorado Springs, CO 80918 U.S.A.

David C. Cook Distribution Canada
55 Woodslee Avenue, Paris, Ontario, Canada N3L 3E5

David C. Cook U.K., Kingsway Communications
Eastbourne, East Sussex BN23 6NT, England

David C. Cook and the graphic circle C logo
are registered trademarks of Cook Communications Ministries.

Unless otherwise indicated, all Scripture quotations are taken from the *New
American Standard Bible*, © Copyright 1960, 1995 by The Lockman
Foundation. Used by permission. Scripture quotations marked NIV are taken
from the *Holy Bible, New International Version®. NIV®*. Copyright © 1973,
1978, 1984 by International Bible Society. Used by permission of
Zondervan. All rights reserved; and KJV are taken from the King James
Version of the Bible. (Public Domain.) Italics in Scripture quotations have
been added by the author for emphasis.

Material from John MacArthur Jr.'s study guides *Spiritual Warfare: Fighting
to Win* (Chicago: Moody Press, 1988) and *The Believer's Armor* (Chicago:
Moody Press, 1986) was used in preparing this book.

LCCN 2006927275
ISBN 978-0-7814-4361-6

© 1992, 1994, 2006 by John MacArthur Jr., second edition,
previous ISBN: 1-56476-016-2
First edition published by Chariot Victor Publishing under
the title *How to Meet the Enemy* © 1992, 1994.

Cover Design: Two Moore Designs/Ray Moore
Cover Photo: © BigStock Photo

Printed in the United States of America
First Printing of Revised Edition, 2006

9 10 11 12 13 14

060611

ACKNOWLEDGMENTS

Thanks to the staff of Grace to You who lent their editorial expertise to this project. Particular thanks to Randy Mellinger, who arranged and edited this book from sermon transcripts.

CONTENTS

჻

INTRODUCTION

> There are two equal and opposite errors into which
> our race can fall about the devils. One is to disbelieve
> in their existence. The other is to believe, and to feel
> an excessive and unhealthy interest in them. They
> themselves are equally pleased by both errors, and hail
> a materialist or magician with the same delight.[1]
>
> —C. S. LEWIS

Lewis was right. Unfortunately, strands of both errors exist in today's church. On the one hand, some Christians are materialists who fail to understand that the Christian life is a fierce spiritual battle.

One reason for a materialistic attitude is indifference. When your world is an easy place to live in, it's easy to forget that a spiritual war is going on. It's easy to forget that millions of souls in the world are in the grasp of Satan. And it's easy to forget that Satan always takes advantage of Christians who are lethargic, indolent, or spiritually stagnant. He loves it when Christians try to hole up in a sanctified environment instead of fighting the battle. Yet that is precisely the agenda of many churches today. People are trying desperately to enjoy fellowship while remaining indifferent to the battle.

Another reason for being materialistic is worldliness. Too many Christians crave earthly, temporal pleasures instead of the rigors of warfare. They seek a life of ease—a life of entertainment and activities, never realizing their role in the battle of the ages. A believer who invests his or her time and resources in mundane things won't understand spiritual warfare.

A Christian who had a deficient view of God's grace said to me, "The wonderful thing about the Christian life is that basically you can do whatever you want." Believers are not handed a free pass to do what they want. They are called to obey Christ, the Commander in Chief. In Matthew 16:24–25, Jesus raised this call: "If anyone wishes to come after Me, he must deny himself, and take up his cross, and follow Me. For whoever wishes to save his life will lose it; but whoever loses his life for My sake will find it."

We can't let spiritual warfare rage around us without joining the fight. It's vital that we take spiritual inventory by asking, *Am I making a difference in the fight?* Too many will settle for indifference and worldliness. Satan has a heyday with such Christians. My prayer is that *your* devotion and commitment level will deepen when you understand how to meet the Enemy.

On the other hand, there are also many in today's church who have an excessive and unhealthy fascination with demons. The following article, which appeared in the *Los Angeles Times*, illustrates this obsession:

> Under the militant banner of "spiritual warfare," growing numbers of evangelical and charismatic Christian leaders are preparing broad assaults on what they call the cosmic powers of darkness.
>
> Fascinated with the notion that Satan commands a hierarchy of territorial demons, some mission agencies and big-church pastors are devising strategies for

"breaking the strongholds" of those evil spirits alleged to be controlling cities and countries.

Some proponents in the fledgling movement already maintain that focused prayer meetings have ended the curse of the Bermuda triangle, led to the 1987 downfall in Oregon of free-love guru Baghwan Shree Rajneesh, and for the 1984 Summer Olympics in Los Angeles, produced a two-week drop in the crime rate, a friendly atmosphere and unclogged freeways.

This is not the cinematic story line for a religious sequel to "Ghostbusters II," yet the developing scenario does have a fictional influence: interest in spiritual warfare has been heightened by two best-selling novels in Christian bookstores. "This Present Darkness," by Frank Peretti, describes the religious fight against "territorial spirits mobilized to dominate a small town." A second Peretti novel has a similar premise.

Fuller Seminary Prof. C. Peter Wagner, who has written extensively on the subject, led a "summit" meeting on cosmic-level spiritual-warfare Monday in Pasadena with two dozen men and women, including a Texas couple heading a group called the "Generals of Intercession" and an Oregon man who conducts "spiritual-warfare boot camps."[2]

More and more Christian leaders seem to be championing such efforts. I know of a large conservative mission organization that is requiring all its missionaries to attend special training seminars to learn how to confront and assault the powers of darkness. Their strategy includes speaking to demons and learning techniques for exorcising them. It is becoming very popular to deliver incantations against Satan and supposedly rebuke or bind him.

What about this fascination? Do believers need to attend spiritual-warfare boot camps? Are we to break the stronghold of demons so we can regain cities and countries? Should believers speak to demons and cast them out? Can we actually bind and rebuke Satan?

Certainly Christians are engaged in a struggle against the powers of darkness, for in Ephesians 6:12, Paul said, "Our struggle is not against flesh and blood, but against the rulers, against the powers, against the world forces of this darkness, against the spiritual forces of wickedness in the heavenly places."

Many of the practices of today's spiritual-warfare movement, however, are in stark contrast to the clear teaching of God's Word. Dr. Archibald Alexander, the first professor of Princeton Seminary and a brilliant theologian, wrote:

> There is nothing more necessary than to distinguish carefully between true and false experiences in religion; to "try the spirits whether they are of God." And in making this discrimination, there is no other test but the infallible Word of God; let every thought, motive, impulse, and emotion be brought to this touchstone. "To the law and the testimony; if they speak not according to these, it is because there is no light in them."[3]

God's Word must be our only guide for all we believe and practice. Let's examine what Scripture says about spiritual warfare in contrast to the beliefs, practices, and experiences of those in today's spiritual-warfare movement.

1

Drawing the Battle Lines

A senator concluded his resignation letter with this honest admission:

> Over a period of years, as I drank the heady wine of power and influence, my priorities in office became distorted. Success and recognition were foremost; honesty and adherence to the law were not at the center of my focus. Like some others before me, I placed undue emphasis on raising funds, on achieving political status and on impressing my friends. Strict compliance with the law would have allowed me to perform my public service without becoming the center of one controversy after another over the years.
>
> I wish my colleagues well and it would please me if someone benefits from what I have said and rededicates himself or herself to staying clear of the line.

When you are willing to walk close to the line, whether
for political success, personal gain or to help your
friends, you risk waking up one day to find out that
you have long since crossed a boundary that you
vowed you would never cross. That is where I find
myself today. Goodbye. Good luck. Thank you. I apol-
ogize. Please include me in your prayers.[1]

The former senator was not the first to drink the heady wine
of power and influence and cross the boundary between right and
wrong. Nor will he be the last. Today many people sacrifice honesty on the altar of prestige, power, and influence. It might seem
hard to believe, but the first crossing of that boundary took place
in heaven.

In the beginning no war or rebellion existed. No one opposed
God's sovereign rule or voiced animosity against His holy purpose
and will. But then a disastrous event occurred, marking the beginning of spiritual warfare.

Thus says the Lord GOD, "You had the seal of perfection, full of wisdom and perfect in beauty. You were in
Eden, the garden of God; every precious stone was
your covering: the ruby, the topaz and the diamond;
the beryl, the onyx and the jasper; the lapis lazuli, the
turquoise and the emerald; and the gold, the work-
manship of your settings and sockets, was in you. On
the day that you were created they were prepared. You
were the anointed cherub who covers, and I placed
you there. You were on the holy mountain of God;
you walked in the midst of the stones of fire. You
were blameless in your ways from the day you were
created until unrighteousness was found in you. By
the abundance of your trade you were internally filled
with violence, and you sinned; therefore I have cast
you as profane from the mountain of God. And I have
destroyed you, O covering cherub, from the midst of

the stones of fire. Your heart was lifted up because of
your beauty; you corrupted your wisdom by reason of
your splendor. I cast you to the ground; I put you
before kings, that they may see you. By the multitude
of your iniquities, in the unrighteousness of your trade
you profaned your sanctuaries. Therefore I have
brought fire from the midst of you; it has consumed
you, and I have turned you to ashes on the earth in
the eyes of all who see you." (Ezek. 28:12–18)

That passage speaks of a being so complete that he possessed
the seal of perfection. It cannot be referring to a mere human
being. Furthermore, in verse 13, the writer said this sublime creature was "in Eden, the garden of God." Clearly, this prophecy is an
indirect reference to Satan, the Serpent—the adversary who was in
the garden of Eden.

In verse 14, the writer identified him as "the anointed cherub
who covers." God designed the ark of the covenant with two
angels—one on each side, spreading their wings over the mercy
seat. These angels were called covering cherubs. They represented
the angels associated with God's holiness, covering the place where
atonement was made between God and man by the sprinkling of
blood. The covering cherubs were subservient to this magnificent
angel, "the anointed cherub"—the highest angelic creature in the
presence of God's full glory and holiness.

Scripture mentions angels and archangels, cherubim and
seraphim, rulers, principalities, and powers. Those terms indicate
that God designed an angelic network to carry out His bidding.
Here, then, was an angel of supreme rank, created by God to be the
anointed cherub.

THE FALL OF SATAN

This highest angel was blameless from the day of his creation. The
day came, however, when unrighteousness was found in him (v.
15). What unrighteousness was specifically found in him? His spirit

of rebellion against God. "Your heart was lifted up because of your beauty" (v. 17) reveals that this archangel allowed his perfection to be the cause of his corruption. That sin was not an inherent part of the being God created, but later issued from within him because of his pride.

Verse 18 was God's response to his sin: "I have brought fire from the midst of you; it has consumed you, and I have turned you to ashes on the earth in the eyes of all who see you." God cast this angel out of heaven to be eventually destroyed.

Isaiah recorded the event.

> How you have fallen from heaven, O star of the morn-
> ing ["Lucifer," KJV], son of the dawn! You have been
> cut down to the earth, you who have weakened the
> nations! But you said in your heart, "I will ascend to
> heaven; I will raise my throne above the stars of God,
> and I will sit on the mount of assembly in the recesses
> of the north. I will ascend above the heights of the
> clouds; I will make myself like the Most High."
> Nevertheless you will be thrust down to Sheol, to the
> recesses of the pit. (Isa. 14:12–15)

The name *Lucifer* means "star of the morning" and "son of the dawn." *Satan* means "accuser." Lucifer became Satan when God cast him out of heaven. "You have been cut down to the earth" (v. 12) speaks of his fall. Jesus said, "I was watching Satan fall from heaven like lightning" (Luke 10:18). The preincarnate Christ was a witness to Satan's fall. Note Lucifer's repeated use of "I will" in Isaiah 14. It reveals his pride, and that pride produced discontent. He wasn't satisfied with being top angel anymore; he wanted to be like God Himself.

In Isaiah 14:15, God responded to Satan's sin: "You will be thrust down to Sheol, to the recesses of the pit." Satan's rebellion will ultimately end in his own destruction. Revelation 20:10 proph-esies Satan's final end: "The devil who deceived them was thrown into the lake of fire and brimstone, where the beast and the false prophet are also; and they will be tormented day and night forever and ever."

THE ARMY OF SATAN

When Satan fell, he did not fall alone. In Revelation 12:4, John said he "swept away a third of the stars of heaven." In verse 9, John identified the stars as fallen angels or demons allied with Satan. Although Satan is a tremendously powerful creature and influences many governments and nations, he is not omnipresent like God. His work is augmented by one-third of the angelic host.

How many is one-third? We don't know. We do know that angels neither procreate nor die (Matt. 22:30). There are as many angels today as in the day of their creation. There's no diminishing or adding to their ranks. Scripture describes the number of holy angels as being "myriads of myriads, and thousands of thousands" (Rev. 5:11). The Greek word for "myriad" means "ten thousand" and was the largest number the language could express. Perhaps there are too many angels to count.

Some of the fallen angels are bound in everlasting chains (Jude v. 6). I believe they were the angels who sinned at the time of the flood as described in Genesis 6:1–7. Because these "sons of God" cohabited with humanity, producing a mixed race, God drowned their offspring in the flood and bound the angels with chains. Perhaps God has put more and more demons into that pit through-out redemptive history. In Luke 8:31, the demons at Gadara "were imploring [Christ] not to command them to go away into the abyss." Other demons are bound temporarily. According to Revelation 9:2, some demons will be released during the tribulation.

Satan's army of demons is highly organized, for believers strug-gle "against the rulers, against the powers, against the world forces of this darkness, against the spiritual forces of wickedness in the heav-enly places" (Eph. 6:12). The Greek construction, using the word translated "against" repeatedly, separates each category of demonic beings—rulers, powers, forces of darkness, and spiritual forces of wickedness. "Rulers" and "powers" obviously refer to demons who have high ranks in the satanic hierarchy. Perhaps "world forces" refers to demons who have infiltrated the political structure of the world and are influencing decisions from behind the scenes. "Darkness" speaks of hell. In Matthew 8:12, Christ called it "outer darkness; in that place there shall be weeping and gnashing of teeth."

People often ask me if I believe there is a global conspiracy of evil organizations trying to gain control of the world. I don't believe there is such a conspiracy on the human level. But I know from Scripture that there is an unseen spiritual global conspiracy involving demons in high places, and many humans and earthly organizations are unwitting participants in it. The Old Testament says that the gods of the nations are demons (cf. Ps. 96:5; 1 Cor. 10:19–20). In 1 John 5:19, John said, "The whole world lies in the power of the evil one." Satan is the god of this world (2 Cor. 4:4), and so he controls much of what occurs in the events of this world.

SATAN'S TARGETS

CHRIST

Christ is Satan's primary target. Why? Because the divine plan was "that through death [Christ] might render powerless him who had the power of death, that is, the devil, and might free those who through fear of death were subject to slavery all their lives" (Heb. 2:14–15). Satan unsuccessfully endeavored to destroy the messianic line so Christ couldn't even be born. At the Savior's birth, King Herod issued a decree to find the Child and slay Him (Matt. 2:16–18). That was a satanic plot. When it didn't work, the Devil tried to conquer Christ in the wilderness (4:1–11). At the cross, perhaps the Devil thought he finally had defeated Christ, but Christ proclaimed His victory over the hellish forces (1 Peter 3:18–20), gloriously rose from the dead, and ascended into heaven.

Satan opposes everything Christ does. Christ revealed the truth (John 1:17), but Satan conceals the truth. In 8:44, Jesus said Satan "does not stand in the truth because there is no truth in him. Whenever he speaks a lie, he speaks from his own nature, for he is a liar and the father of lies."

Christ gives life, but Satan takes life. The one who trusts in Christ as Savior and Lord "has passed out of death into life" (5:24). However, Satan "was a murderer from the beginning" (8:44) and has "the power of death" (Heb. 2:14).

Christ produces spiritual fruit in our lives: love, joy, peace, patience, kindness, goodness, faithfulness, gentleness, and self-control (Gal. 5:22–23). But Satan loves the fleshly fruit of "immorality, impurity, sensuality, idolatry, sorcery, enmities, strife, jealousy, outbursts of anger, disputes, dissensions, factions, envying, drunkenness, carousing, and things like these" (vv. 19–21).

Christ permits tests or trials in our lives to help us grow spiritually (James 1:3), but Satan lures us with temptation to destroy us (1 Peter 5:8). Christ sets believers free (John 8:31–32), but Satan enslaves the lost (2 Tim. 2:26). Christ defends believers (1 John 2:1), but Satan accuses them (Rev. 12:10).

Today Satan continues to oppose the work of Christ. He will fight against Christ when He returns and will finally be dealt with when he is cast eternally into the lake of fire.

HOLY ANGELS

Holy angels are another target of Satan and his demons. A holy angel appeared to Daniel and said:

> Do not be afraid, Daniel, for from the first day that you set your heart on understanding this [information regarding Israel's future] and on humbling yourself before your God, your words were heard, and I have come in response to your words. But the prince of the kingdom of Persia was withstanding me for twenty-one days; then behold, Michael, one of the chief princes, came to help me, for I had been left there with the kings of Persia. Now I have come to give you an understanding of what will happen to your people in the latter days, for the vision pertains to the days yet future. (Dan. 10:12–14)

Daniel had set his heart on understanding why his people had not returned to Israel, so he fasted and prayed for a lengthy period of time (vv. 2–3). A holy angel appeared to assure him that God was not indifferent to his prayers. God had heard them on the first day, but delivery of His answer was delayed for twenty-one days.

The angel explained that the "prince of the kingdom of Persia" had detained him (v. 13). The context reveals the prince spoken of here was not a man. No mere man could withstand an angelic being. Perhaps this was a demon indwelling the king of Persia. His position was to influence the events in Persia and hinder God's plans for Israel's future. His relationship with Persia was ongoing; he would fight the angel again later on (v. 20).

God sent the archangel Michael to release the unnamed angel from conflict (v. 13). Michael is mentioned two other times in the Old Testament (10:21; 12:1) and twice in the New Testament (Jude v. 9; Rev. 12:7). It seems God has given him the special responsibility of guarding Israel. Apparently God has assigned certain holy angels to specific nations to carry out His purposes. Possibly Michael is the highest of the angels. He and the holy angel fought against the demon prince of Persia. Together they were victorious.

Once the Persian conflict ended, the holy messenger would begin fighting the prince of Greece—the next great world power (Dan. 10:20). Satan works at the highest levels, trying to thwart God's divine program. When Persia was in power, apparently Satan assigned a demon to that empire to influence its affairs against God. About two centuries later, when Greece came to power, he would assign another demon to that nation. This holy messenger would be there to fight against them, and Michael would be available to give help at any time (v. 21).

The book of Jude provides another glimpse of cosmic conflict. In verse 9, Jude says, "Michael the archangel, when he disputed with the devil and argued about the body of Moses, did not dare pronounce against him a railing judgment, but said, 'The Lord rebuke you!'" Why did the Devil want the body of Moses? We really don't know. Perhaps he wanted to display the body, so people would worship it as an idol. Throughout history people have worshipped artifacts. Whatever the reason, Michael appealed to the Lord Himself. Unlike so many "experts" in spiritual warfare today, Michael did not rail at the Devil or rebuke him. He invoked the Lord's name. Evidently he prevailed in the conflict. In Deuteronomy 34:6, the writer said that the Lord buried Moses "in the valley in the land of Moab, opposite Beth-peor; but no man knows his burial place to this day."

ISRAEL

Throughout history the powers of darkness have furiously tried to wipe out the nation of Israel, knowing it is crucial to God's eternal plan because of the covenant He made with Abraham. Israel's history is a chronicle of persecution and holocaust. The mass murder of Jews under Hitler's regime was only the latest in many centuries of demonically motivated persecution. During the great tribulation, a holocaust of even greater proportion will exist on earth as Satan attacks Israel, but God will supernaturally protect her (Rev. 12:4–6).

BELIEVERS

Believers are yet another target of Satan. In Revelation 12:10 a loud voice in heaven proclaimed, "The accuser of our brethren has been thrown down, he who accuses them before our God day and night." Satan brings vicious accusations—and so much more than that—against all who believe in Christ. We'll take a closer look at that conflict in the remaining chapters of this book.

What is spiritual warfare? A war of universal proportions pitting God and His truth against Satan and his lies. It's a battle of wills between God and Satan. It's a cosmic conflict that involves God and the highest creature He ever made, and it filters down to every human being. Satan and his army of demons are fighting Christ, His holy angels, the nation of Israel, and believers. The battle lines are clearly drawn.

SATAN AS GOD'S INSTRUMENT

༄

Can demons inhabit or spatially indwell a believer? Most proponents of today's spiritual-warfare movement think they can. Professor C. Fred Dickason wrote, "A genuine Christian may become possessed at least to some degree, even to the point where they speak with strange voices or in foreign languages."[1]

In a sequel to that book he prefers the term *demonization* (with an emphasis on control) over *demon possession* (with an emphasis on ownership), explaining himself in this way: "Demonization is always presented [in the Bible] as a spirit's inhabiting a human."[2] So Dr. Dickason claims that a believer can be owned by God yet inhabited by demons.

He concedes that you can't look to the Bible to support that assertion.[3] In his attempt to secure proof, Dickason turned to clinical observations to help decide the issue. By relying on his own counseling experience and that of others (which allegedly included conversations between the counselors and demons), he concluded,

"Having researched the evidence in broad fashion by proper application of both biblical and clinical parameters, we may come to the valid conclusion that Christians can be demonized."[4] Later in his book he also wrote, "The first and most basic result of deliverance of the demonized is the removal of the wicked spirits that were inhabiting the person."[5] He is not alone in his view, for another professor, Merrill Unger, declared:

> Who dares assert that a demon spirit will not invade
> the life of a believer in which the Holy Spirit has
> been grieved by serious and persistent sin and
> quenched by flagrant disobedience? ... A demon ...
> enters as a squatter and an intruder, and is subject
> to momentary eviction.... Only as the believer fails
> to walk by faith does he fall into sin, which if it is
> not confessed and curbed, may ultimately result in
> the forfeiture of the Spirit's power to shield him
> from demonic invasion.[6]

Those excerpts reflect the typical position of those in today's spiritual-warfare movement. Inevitably, however, those who teach that demons can indwell believers are forced to find support for their view in subjective experiences rather than the clear teaching of God's Word.

THE TOUCHSTONE OF TRUTH

It is unacceptable to rely on clinical data and conversations with demons in lieu of scriptural teaching. Jonathan Edwards, who was one of America's greatest theologians, correctly wrote:

> Spiritual understanding sees what is actually in
> Scripture; it does not make a new meaning for it.
> Making a new meaning for Scripture is equivalent to
> making a new Scripture! It is adding to God's Word, a
> practice God condemns (Prov. 30:6)....

A large part of the false religion in the world is made up of ... experiences and the false notion they excite. Non-Christian religions are full of them. So (unfortunately) is the history of the Church. These experiences captivate people so Satan transforms himself into an angel of light, deceives multitudes, and corrupts true religion. Church leaders must be constantly on their guard against these delusions.[7]

God's Word is our only reliable source of truth about Satan and demons. Princeton theologian and scholar Dr. Charles Hodge rightly warned:

No amount of learning, no superiority of talent, nor even the pretension to inspiration, can justify a departure from the ... truths taught by men to whose inspiration God has borne witness. All teachers must be brought to this standard; and even if an angel from heaven should teach anything contrary to the Scriptures, he should be regarded as anathema, Gal. 1:8. It is a matter of constant gratitude that we have such a standard whereby to try the spirits whether they be of God.[8]

What does God's Word, the touchstone of truth, say? Can demons inhabit or spatially indwell a true believer? Can they walk through an open door and become a squatter? Proponents of today's spiritual-warfare movement say yes, but they base their answer on subjective experience, not on God's Word. The Bible makes it clear that such a claim has no justifiable basis.

There is no clear example in the Bible where a demon ever inhabited or invaded a true believer. Never in the New Testament epistles are believers warned about the possibility of being inhabited by demons. Neither do we see anyone rebuking, binding, or casting demons out of a true believer. The Epistles never instruct believers to cast out demons, whether from a believer or unbeliever.

In every instance when Christ and the apostles cast out demons, the demon-possessed people were unbelievers.

The collective teaching of Scripture is that demons can never spatially indwell a true believer. A clear implication of 2 Corinthians 6, for example, is that the indwelling Holy Spirit could never cohabit with demons:

> What harmony has Christ with Belial, or what has a
> believer in common with an unbeliever? Or what agree-
> ment has the temple of God with idols? For we are the
> temple of the living God; just as God said, "I will dwell
> in them and walk among them; and I will be their God,
> and they shall be My people." (vv. 15–16)

In Colossians 1:13, Paul said God "rescued us from the domain of darkness, and transferred us to the kingdom of His beloved Son." Salvation brings true deliverance and protection from Satan. In Romans 8:37, Paul said we overwhelmingly conquer through Christ. In 1 Corinthians 15:57, he said God gives us the victory. In 2 Corinthians 2:14, he said God always leads us in triumph. In 1 John 2:13, John said we have overcome the Evil One. And, in 4:4, he said the indwelling Holy Spirit is greater than Satan. How could anyone affirm those glorious truths yet believe demons can indwell genuine believers?

THE TRUE MEANING OF CONVERSION

Many of the leading voices in today's spiritual-warfare movement are too quick to hail every profession of faith in Christ as proof of salvation. That reflects the easy-believism that has swept this generation.

A thorough biblical understanding of the doctrine of conversion makes it clear that demons could never indwell or possess a believer. Jonathan Edwards wrote about true conversion:

Scripture describes conversion in terms which imply or signify a change of nature: being born again, becoming new creatures, rising from the dead, being renewed in the spirit of the mind, dying to sin and living to righteousness, putting off the old man and putting on the new, becoming partakers of the divine nature, and so on.

It follows that if there is no real and lasting change in people who think they are converted, their religion is worthless, whatever their experiences may be. Conversion is the turning of the whole man from sin to God. God can restrain unconverted people from sin, of course, but in conversion he turns the very heart and nature from sin to holiness. The converted person becomes the enemy of sin.

What, then, shall we make of a person who says he has experienced conversion, but whose religious emotions soon die away, leaving him much the same person as he was before? He seems as selfish, worldly, foolish, perverse and un-Christian as ever. This speaks against him louder than any religious experiences can speak for him.

In Christ Jesus, neither circumcision nor uncircumcision, neither a dramatic experience nor a quiet one, neither a wonderful testimony nor a dull one, counts for anything. The only thing that counts is a new creation.[9]

In Matthew 12, Christ rebuked those who were following Him just for the sake of witnessing great signs and wonders:

> When the unclean spirit goes out of a man, it passes through waterless places seeking rest, and does not find it. Then it says, "I will return to my house from which I came"; and when it comes, it finds it unoccupied, swept, and put in order. Then it goes and takes along with it seven other spirits more wicked than itself, and they go in and live there; and the last

state of that man becomes worse than the first. That
is the way it will also be with this evil generation.
(vv. 43–45)

Instead of responding with spectacular signs and wonders,
Christ addressed their need for salvation. Many people appear to
have their lives in order. But in reality, they have not trusted Christ
as Savior and Lord. Their souls are "unoccupied"—that is, the
Holy Spirit does not indwell them. Thus they are open to demonic
invasion. That cannot be true of those whose bodies are temples of
the Holy Spirit (cf. 2 Cor. 6:16).

According to 1 Peter 1:5, when Christ reigns in a person's
life, that person is kept by God's power. As a result, "the evil one
does not touch him" (1 John 5:18). When the Holy Spirit inhab-
its a person, no demon can set up house as a squatter. Indwelling
by demons is only evidence of a lack of genuine salvation.

ALL THINGS FOR GOOD

Although demons cannot inhabit believers, God sometimes permits
Satan to afflict Christians externally with adversity. We will not
always know the reason, but we do know that God sovereignly controls every situation to accomplish His purposes, causing all such
adversity to work for the believer's good (Rom. 8:28). Let's look at
some biblical examples of how that is so.

THE PERSEVERANCE OF JOB

The book of Job is the classic illustration of how God sometimes
permits Satan to afflict His own. It takes us behind the earthly scene
to this remarkable exchange between God and Satan in heaven:

The LORD said to Satan, "From where do you
come?" Then Satan answered the LORD and said,
"From roaming about on the earth and walking

around on it." And the LORD said to Satan, "Have
you considered My servant Job? For there is no
one like him on the earth, a blameless and upright
man, fearing God and turning away from evil."
Then Satan answered the LORD, "Does Job fear
God for nothing? Have You not made a hedge
about him and his house and all that he has, on
every side? You have blessed the work of his hands,
and his possessions have increased in the land. But
put forth Your hand now and touch all that he has;
he will surely curse You to Your face." Then the
LORD said to Satan, "Behold, all that he has is in
your power, only do not put forth your hand on
him." So Satan departed from the presence of the
LORD. (1:7–12)

Job was a righteous man whom God blessed with abundant
wealth: 7,000 sheep, 3,000 camels, 500 yoke of oxen, 500 don-
keys, and many servants. According to verse 3, he "was the greatest
of all the men of the east."

Satan came before God in heaven and accused Job of serving
the Lord for selfish reasons—for protection and prosperity. Satan
challenged God to take away all Job's temporal blessings, hoping
that would prove the hypocrisy in Job's heart. God accepted the
challenge and permitted Satan to afflict Job. He was allowed to
take away Job's possessions but was prohibited from harming Job
himself.

Disaster soon followed. Fire fell from heaven and killed Job's
sheep. Raiders captured his camels, killing all but one servant in
the process. Satan ended with what he hoped would be his
knockout punch: While Job's children were dining together, "a
great wind came from across the wilderness and struck the four
corners of the house, and it fell on the young people and they
died" (v. 19). It was a cruel calamity that was intended to break
Job's faith.

Yet Job didn't respond the way Satan hoped. Rather, "Job
arose and tore his robe and shaved his head, and he fell to the

ground and worshiped. He said, 'Naked I came from my mother's womb, and naked I shall return there. The LORD gave and the LORD has taken away. Blessed be the name of the LORD.' Through all this Job did not sin nor did he blame God" (vv. 20–22). Job bowed to the Lord in prayer and worship, accepting God's sovereign design and purpose, even though he didn't know why he was suffering.

J. I. Packer has written:

> This is the ultimate reason, from our standpoint, why God fills our lives with troubles and perplexities of one sort and another—it is to ensure that we shall learn to hold Him fast. The reason why the Bible spends so much of its time reiterating that God is a strong rock, a firm defense, and a sure refuge and help for the weak, is that God spends so much of His time bringing home to us that we are weak, both mentally and morally, and dare not trust ourselves to find, or to follow, the right road.... God wants us to feel that our way through life is rough and perplexing, so that we may learn to lean on Him. Therefore He takes steps to drive us out of self-confidence to trust in Himself.[10]

But Satan wasn't through:

> Again there was a day when the sons of God came to present themselves before the LORD, and Satan also came among them to present himself before the LORD.... The LORD said to Satan, "Have you considered My servant Job? For there is no one like him on the earth, a blameless and upright man fearing God and turning away from evil. And he still holds fast his integrity, although you incited Me against him to ruin him without cause." Satan answered the

LORD and said, "Skin for skin! Yes, all that a man
has he will give for his life. However, put forth Your
hand now, and touch his bone and his flesh; he will
curse You to Your face." So the LORD said to Satan,
"Behold, he is in your power, only spare his life."
Then Satan went out from the presence of the
LORD. (2:1, 3–7)

Satan accused Job of remaining faithful to God to protect his
health. Once again God permitted Satan to afflict Job, but was
restricted from taking Job's life. Satan plagued Job with painful
oozing sores from the soles of his feet to the top of his head (v. 7).
His condition was so deplorable that his wife urged him to curse
God, but he refused to do so (v. 10).

Job still did not know why he was suffering. He cried out, "Oh
that I knew where I might find Him [the Lord], that I might come
to His seat! I would present my case before Him and fill my mouth
with arguments" (23:3–4). But heaven remained silent. Job was
unaware of the scenes being played out in that realm between Satan
and God. Later the Lord did answer him out of a whirlwind, but
even then Job was not informed of the reason for his suffering.

The typical counselor today would probably advise Job to say,
"Satan, I bind you!" But though Job was the choicest of God's servants, his sufferings were part of God's plan. Surely that is also true
of many who suffer today. Can today's spiritual-warfare "experts"
simply bypass the Lord's sovereign purposes and rebuke Satan? Of
course not.

Can afflictions from Satan actually benefit the true believer?
Yes! Job, for example, came away with an increased awareness of
God's greatness and his own sinfulness (40:4–5). He also learned
the necessity of submitting to God's sovereign purposes no matter
what the cost might be (42:2–6). Gleason Archer had this keen
insight in his commentary on Job:

This record shows that there were in fact high and
noble purposes achieved through submitting him to all

of the calamities he had to endure. He had been greatly honored by being chosen especially by God to demonstrate the meaning of full surrender. Satan had challenged the Lord to prove that Job's piety was based on something higher than self-interest....

It was a great honor indeed for Job to be chosen to prove that Satan was wrong on this very important point. Had Job been informed in advance that his coming ordeal was intended to serve this high and holy purpose, he would have found it much easier to bear his trials with cheerfulness and fortitude. But had he been so informed in advance, the test would have been invalidated. Why? Because it was essential for the victim of these trials to trust God and continue to submit to Him through them all, even though he lacked the slightest clue as to why a hitherto protective and loving God should appear to forsake him so completely to the malignity of Satan.[11]

You may be suffering or know someone who is, but you have no clue as to why. By looking to the example of Job, you can find comfort, encouragement, and hope. The apostle Peter wrote, "Therefore those also who suffer according to the will of God shall entrust their souls to a faithful Creator" (1 Peter 4:19). May the Lord help us cultivate that attitude as a way of life.

PAUL'S THORN

The Lord also permitted Satan to afflict the apostle Paul. On three occasions Paul received a vision of the resurrected Christ. He evidently struggled with pride, for he said, "Because of the surpassing greatness of the revelations, for this reason, to keep me from exalting myself, there was given me a thorn in the flesh, a messenger of Satan to torment me—to keep me from exalting myself!" (2 Cor. 12:7).

Paul received a thorn in the flesh. Many have made various suggestions for the thorn's identity—a troublesome individual, persecution, Paul's physical appearance, epilepsy, malaria, or even an eye disease. What was the thorn? We really don't know. Whatever it was, it was painful, because the Greek word for "torment" refers to bone-crushing blows of the fist. Since Paul's painful thorn was pummeling him, three times he asked the Lord to remove it (v. 8).

Note that Paul didn't attempt to bind, rebuke, or cast out this satanic messenger. He simply prayed to the Lord for its removal. Certainly God was able to do as Paul prayed, but He chose not to (v. 9). Jerry Bridges made this observation:

> God in His infinite wisdom knows exactly what adversity we need to grow more and more into the likeness of His Son. He not only knows what we need but when we need it and how best to bring it to pass in our lives. He is the perfect teacher or coach. His discipline is always exactly suited for our needs. He never over trains us by allowing too much adversity in our lives.[12]

Paul willingly accepted God's design for his life: "Most gladly, therefore, I will rather boast about my weaknesses, so that the power of Christ may dwell in me. Therefore I am well content with weaknesses, with insults, with distresses, with persecutions, with difficulties, for Christ's sake; for when I am weak, then I am strong" (vv. 9–10).

If it were possible to remove the thorn in the flesh by saying, "Messenger of Satan, I bind you," God's plan could have been foiled. In the end, Paul was glad for this affliction because it helped him grow spiritually.

THE SIFTING OF PETER

In Luke 22:31–32, Christ said to Peter, "Satan has demanded permission to sift you like wheat; but I have prayed for you, that your faith may not fail; and you, when once you have turned again, strengthen your brothers."

Satan wanted Peter because he was crucial to the early church's development. When Peter heard that Satan was after him, he responded, "Lord, with You I am ready to go both to prison and to death!" (v. 33) Later that same evening, Peter denied Christ three times. Afterward he "went out and wept bitterly" (v. 62). That was evidence of his repentance and restoration to God.

What did Peter learn as a result of Satan's sifting? That he could not stand on his own. It also made him a more useful vessel for God because Christ told him to strengthen others after his repentance (v. 32). Peter well knew the value of the refining process, for years later he wrote this to persecuted believers:

> In this you greatly rejoice, even though now for a little while, if necessary, you have been distressed by various trials, so that the proof of your faith, being more precious than gold which is perishable, even though tested by fire, may be found to result in praise and glory and honor at the revelation of Jesus Christ. (1 Peter 1:6–7)

God used Satan's afflicting hand for the spiritual benefit of Job, Paul, and Peter. None of them sought to command, rebuke, or bind Satan. For them the real issue was not the activity of Satan, but the accomplishment of God's sovereign purposes. Our attitude should be no different.

THE JUDGMENT OF GOD

Sometimes God's purposes are not so benign. Scripture reveals He will actually hand people over to Satan to punish them for their sin and disobedience. Let's look at a few examples.

SAUL'S TORMENT

Scripture tells us that "an evil spirit from the LORD terrorized" King Saul (1 Sam. 16:14). Now that doesn't mean the Lord is evil or that evil spirits regularly dwell in His presence. It simply refers to a demon who received the Lord's permission to terrorize Saul. Neither Satan nor his demons can function apart from God's permissive will.

Why did the Lord permit a demon to torment Saul? Because Saul wanted to follow his own way instead of God's. An example of that occurred in 1 Samuel 13. The prophet Samuel instructed Saul to wait seven days for him to arrive at Gilgal, where he would then present an offering to God and give Saul instructions about an upcoming battle with the Philistines. However, Samuel did not come immediately after the seven days. Perhaps he was testing Saul to see if he would obey God's instructions. There is no indication of Saul's seeking guidance through Scripture or prayer during the waiting period.

What happened next? Saul took it upon himself to make the offering to God (vv. 9–10). That was a serious sin, for only those chosen by the Lord could serve as priests (Num. 16:40; 18:1–7). Samuel arrived just as Saul completed the offering, and this exchange took place:

Samuel: What have you done?

Saul: Because I saw that the people were scattering from me, and that you did not come within the appointed days, and that the Philistines were assembling at Michmash, therefore I said, "Now the Philistines will come down against me at Gilgal, and I have not asked the favor of the LORD." So *I forced myself* and offered the burnt offering.

Samuel: You have acted foolishly; you have not kept the commandment of the LORD your God, which He commanded you, for now the LORD would have established your kingdom over Israel forever. But now your kingdom shall not endure. The LORD has sought out for Himself a man after His own heart, and the LORD has

> appointed him as ruler over His people, because
> you have not kept what the LORD commanded
> you. (1 Sam. 13:11–14)

Because Saul made excuses for his sin and did not repent, the kingdom passed to David.

How was Saul's torment from the evil spirit manifested? By his desire to see David dead. David had already received divine enabling to accomplish the responsibilities God had set before him (16:13). But since the Spirit of God had departed from Saul (v. 14), he undoubtedly lost both the desire and ability to function effectively as king. As a result, David's popularity steadily grew in Israel. In 1 Samuel 18:6–9, the writer said:

> It happened as they were coming, when David
> returned from killing the Philistine, that the women
> came out of all the cities of Israel, singing and danc-
> ing, to meet King Saul, with tambourines, with joy
> and with musical instruments. The women sang as
> they played, and said, "Saul has slain his thousands,
> and David his ten thousands." Then Saul became very
> angry, for this saying displeased him; and he said,
> "They have ascribed to David ten thousands, but to
> me they have ascribed thousands. Now what more can
> he have but the kingdom?" Saul looked at David with
> suspicion from that day on.

Saul was jealous. And he was painfully aware that God's blessing on David's life paralleled his own demise.

The story continues:

> It came about on the next day that an evil spirit from
> God came mightily upon Saul, and he raved in the
> midst of the house, while David was playing the harp
> with his hand, as usual; and a spear was in Saul's
> hand. Saul hurled the spear for he thought, "I will

pin David to the wall." But David escaped from his
presence twice.

Now Saul was afraid of David, for the LORD was
with him but had departed from Saul. (vv. 10–12)

David was ministering in the court of Saul. When the demon
came upon Saul, he lost control of himself. David was summoned
to soothe him with music. Under the demon's influence, however,
Saul threw a javelin at David, hoping to fulfill the wicked desire that
had seized him.

The story of Saul goes from bad to worse. Saul was so out of
control that he stripped himself naked and fell to the floor in a stupor (19:22–24), massacred a group of priests for helping David
(22:6–19), and consulted a medium to speak with the dead
(28:7–20). In the end he committed suicide. Perhaps you're wondering, "Isn't Saul an example of a believer indwelt by demons?"
No. The question of whether Saul was genuinely a believer has
been debated by Bible students. The best we can say is that
Scripture is ambiguous regarding Saul's eternal destiny. Moreover,
while Saul was troubled and tragically influenced by a demon,
nothing indicates that he was indwelt or demonically possessed. He
cannot be cited as biblical proof that believers can be indwelt by evil
spirits. God turned him over to Satan as judgment for his sin.

JUDAS'S SATANIC BETRAYAL

In the upper room just before His crucifixion, Christ told His
disciples that one of them would betray Him (John 13:21). When
the disciples asked the Lord to identify the person, Christ responded:

"[The betrayer] is the one for whom I shall dip the
morsel and give it to him." So when He had dipped
the morsel, He took and gave it to Judas, the son of
Simon Iscariot. And after the morsel, Satan then
entered into him. Therefore Jesus said to him, "What
you do, do quickly." (vv. 26–27)

Judas had been with Christ for three years, observing His works and listening to His words. He was aware of Christ's perfection and power but refused to repent and believe in Christ for salvation. God therefore turned him over to Satan. A parallel passage in the book of Luke says:

> Satan entered into Judas who was called Iscariot,
> belonging to the number of the twelve. And he went
> away and discussed with the chief priests and officers
> how he might betray Him to them. They were glad,
> and agreed to give him money. (22:3–5)

Under Satan's influence, Judas sold out Christ.

> Satan himself makes Judas his tool by filling his mind
> with traitorous thoughts and moving his will to act
> on them. This is mental possession, giving Satan con-
> trol of the mind, heart, and will. "Satan entered into
> Judas" by no compulsion but as a welcome master
> who is received by a willing slave.[13]

Judas came to the same miserable end as Saul by committing suicide.

THE INCESTUOUS CORINTHIAN

Does God use Satan as His instrument to judge certain people in the church? Yes. Paul wrote to the church at Corinth, "It is actually reported that there is immorality among you, and immorality of such a kind as does not exist even among the Gentiles, that someone has his father's wife" (1 Cor. 5:1). "Father's wife" probably indicates that the woman was his stepmother, not his mother. In either case, how-ever, it was an incestuous relationship in God's eyes (Lev. 18:7–8).

Incredibly the Corinthian believers, instead of mourning over this obviously immoral situation, were actually proud of it (v. 2)!

Paul responded with this admonition: "Deliver such a one to Satan for the destruction of his flesh, so that his spirit may be saved in the day of the Lord Jesus" (v. 5).

What does delivering the offender to Satan mean? It means putting the guilty one out of the church, thus stripping him of the protection of the fellowship. In verse 2, Paul plainly said the offender was to be removed from their midst. He was to be cut off from the community of God's children and the Lord's Table.

Paul underscored the importance of church discipline by using an analogy:

> Do you not know that a little leaven leavens the whole
> lump of dough? Clean out the old leaven so that you
> may be a new lump, just as you are in fact unleavened.
> For Christ our Passover also has been sacrificed.
> Therefore let us celebrate the feast, not with old leaven,
> nor with the leaven of malice and wickedness, but with
> the unleavened bread of sincerity and truth. (vv. 6–8)

Leaven represents sin, and the dough represents the church. If given the opportunity, sin will permeate a whole church just as leaven permeates a whole loaf of bread. By its very nature sin ferments, corrupts, and spreads. But Christ, God's perfect Passover Lamb, separates us from the dominion of sin. Therefore, we are to remove everything from the old life that would permeate the new. We are to eat the bread of honesty, integrity, and truth, not wickedness.

Paul then applied the analogy to the Corinthians:

> I wrote to you not to associate with any so-called
> brother if he is an immoral person, or covetous, or an
> idolater, or a reviler, or a drunkard, or a swindler—not
> even to eat with such a one.... Remove the wicked
> man from among yourselves. (vv. 11, 13)

Jesus made it clear that when a person *claims* to be a believer but continues in sin and ignores what the church has to say, he or she is to be put out of that fellowship and regarded as an unbeliever (Matt. 18:15–17). That places the sinning person under Satan's full control. First John 5:19 says, "The whole world lies in the power of the evil one." The world is already in Satan's hands because of sin. Since the church is the object of God's care, love, and blessing, it is insulated and protected. Church discipline removes sinning members from that protection, leaving them exposed to Satan.

Paul said the Corinthian offender was to be delivered to Satan for "the destruction of his flesh" (1 Cor. 5:5). That may refer to illness or to physical death. In any case, Paul's instruction certainly differs from the practices of the modern spiritual-warfare movement. Rather than delivering people from Satan, he said that the church sometimes has the responsibility of delivering a person to Satan! Now that's a form of "deliverance ministry" few speak about today.

Was the incestuous man a believer or unbeliever? We really don't know. Paul simply characterized him as a "so-called brother" (v. 11).

Sometimes the Lord uses means other than church discipline to put people out of the church. Perhaps you know individuals who withdrew from church involvement, but you never knew why. Then later you heard that their lives were in shambles, marred by broken marriages, immorality, or drunkenness. Perhaps God was purging them from the church because of sin.

THE SHIPWRECK OF HYMENAEUS AND ALEXANDER

Besides 1 Corinthians 5, 1 Timothy 1 is the only other place where Paul speaks of delivering someone over to Satan. He said to Timothy:

> Fight the good fight, keeping faith and a good con-
> science, which some have rejected and suffered shipwreck
> in regard to their faith. Among these are Hymenaeus and
> Alexander, whom I have handed over to Satan, so that
> they will be taught not to blaspheme. (vv. 18–20)

"Keeping faith" refers to believing the truth and holding to it. It is a lifetime commitment to believe God's truth. "A good conscience" speaks of a pure moral standing before God and man.

According to verse 19, some people rejected both those things. Who were they? They were leaders in the church at Ephesus and perhaps in surrounding churches (vv. 3–7). They rejected God's Word for a system that would allow them to lie for their own lust and gratification. As a result, they "suffered shipwreck." Those words picture a ship being dashed into pieces. They speak of destruction in the spiritual and moral realms. Paul identified two men who suffered such a fate: Hymenaeus and Alexander. We cannot say for certain if they were believers or unbelievers.

How did Paul respond? He delivered them over to Satan. That is, he disciplined them out of the church "that they will be taught not to blaspheme" (v. 20). The Greek word for "taught" speaks of physically inflicted punishment. The same word is used elsewhere in Scripture of the sickness and death brought upon those who abused the Lord's Table (1 Cor. 11:32). What was the purpose of such judgment? To teach them not to slander God through false teaching and unholy living. Dr. Homer Kent wrote:

Excommunication from the church [church discipline] places the offender back in the world which is Satan's domain. Hence to deliver unto Satan can be understood as removal back to the world.... Such a removal from the church was corrective in its intent. If the false teachers were allowed to continue in their evil practices, they would not only lead others astray, but would delude themselves into a false sense of spiritual security. But removal into Satan's realm would cause the offenders to face the issues. If they were truly saved, the buffeting by Satan would cause them to see their error and forsake their sin.[14]

THE LIE OF ANANIAS AND SAPPHIRA

In Acts 5:1–11, we learn of two professing believers in the early church who were turned over to Satan:

> A man named Ananias, with his wife Sapphira, sold a piece of property, and kept back some of the price for himself, with his wife's full knowledge, and bringing a portion of it, he laid it at the apostles' feet. But Peter said, "Ananias, why has Satan filled your heart to lie to the Holy Spirit and to keep back some of the price of the land? While it remained unsold, did it not remain your own? And after it was sold, was it not under your control? Why is it that you have conceived this deed in your heart? You have not lied to men but to God." And as he heard these words, Ananias fell down and breathed his last; and great fear came over all who heard of it. The young men got up and covered him up, and after carrying him out, they buried him. Now there elapsed an interval of about three hours, and his wife came in, not knowing what had happened. And Peter responded to her, "Tell me whether you sold the land for such and such a price?" And she said, "Yes, that was the price." Then Peter said to her, "Why is it that you have agreed together to put the Spirit of the Lord to the test? Behold, the feet of those who have buried your husband are at the door, and they shall carry you out as well." And immediately she fell at his feet and breathed her last, and the young men came in and found her dead, and they carried her out and buried her beside her husband. And great fear came over the whole church, and over all who heard of these things.

It's apparent that Ananias and Sapphira had promised the Lord they would give Him all the proceeds from the property they sold. Instead they kept back part of the profit, in essence lying to the Holy Spirit. They laid what they claimed to be the entire price at the apostles' feet. Because of their lie, they were struck dead.

This was the ultimate excommunication! Were Ananias and Sapphira true Christians? Scripture doesn't say. In what sense did Satan fill their hearts? Were they possessed by him? Again, Scripture does not spell the answers out for us. Satan surely filled their hearts with evil thoughts, lies, and covetousness. Whether he took up residence himself is not stated. Though some will point to Ananias and Sapphira as examples of saints who were indwelt or controlled by Satan, there is no warrant for that from the text.

Like the others we have seen, Ananias and Sapphira were judged by God's granting Satan permission to deal with them.

Although Satan and demons cannot inhabit a true believer, God can use them to discipline unrepentant Christians for their sin. That clearly reveals God's attitude toward sin and protects the purity of the church. How can you avoid judgment for sin? Not by saying, "Satan, I bind you." Not by commanding demons, but by simply receiving the truth of God's Word and reflecting the holiness of Christ.

If you are a true believer, please take to heart these encouraging words from a Puritan saint:

> God has thoughts of love in all He does to His people.
> The ground of His dealings with us is love (though the
> occasion may be sin), the manner of His dealings is
> love, and the purpose of His dealings is love. He has
> regard, in all, to our good here, to make us partakers
> of His holiness, and to our glory hereafter, to make us
> partakers of His glory.[15]

Paul expressed the same thought in this way: "We know that God causes all things to work together for good to those who love God, to those who are called according to His purpose. For those whom He foreknew, He also predestined to become conformed to the image of His Son" (Rom. 8:28–29).

3

SATAN ATTACKS
THE CHURCH

ᘯ

Frank Peretti's best-selling novels *This Present Darkness* and *Piercing the Darkness* have added fuel to the fire of today's spiritual-warfare movement. His stories tell of Christians fighting with packs of demons who take over towns and infiltrate the government, educational system, and churches.

Unfortunately, many leading advocates of the spiritual-warfare movement seem to take such fiction as fact. They assert that believers are to seek out and confront demons associated with specific cities, neighborhoods, and other specific areas and locations. They call this "territorial warfare." One advocate, Timothy Warner, wrote:

> I have come to believe that Satan does indeed assign a
> demon or a corps of demons to every geopolitical unit
> in the world and that they are among the principalities
> and powers against whom we wrestle.[1]

In *Charisma and the Christian Life* an article recounted one pastor's experience in such warfare:

> *Evanston, Illinois.* Steve Nicholson has preached the gospel in the area for six years, with virtually no fruit.... Nicholson begins some serious prayer and fasting.
>
> A grotesque, unnatural being appears to him. It growls, "Why are you bothering me?" It identifies itself as a demon of witchcraft who has dominion over the geographical area.
>
> In the heat of warfare, Nicholson names the city streets in the surrounding area. The spirit retorts, "I don't want to give you that much." In the name of Jesus, Nicholson commands the spirit to give up the territory.
>
> During the next three months the church doubles in size from 70 to 150, mostly from new converts out of witchcraft. Nearly all of the new believers must be delivered from demons.[2]

Another leader in the movement warned,

> Dealing with territorial spirits is major league warfare and should not be undertaken casually. I know few who have the necessary expertise, and if you do not know what you are doing, Satan will eat you for breakfast.[3]

Certainly Satan's army of demons is organized (Eph. 6:12), and as we have noted, Daniel 10 does give evidence of conflict between a demon and holy angels over territory. But does that mean the church is to wage turf wars with Satan? Can we simply name the streets in our city and evict a demon from his geographical dominion by invoking Jesus' name? Certainly not. Those kind of incantations have no biblical basis.

The battle in Daniel 10 was fought in heaven, not on earth. It involved two angels and one demon, no humans. When the angel needed help against the prince of the kingdom of Persia, what did God do? Did He ask Daniel to pray for that angel and bind the demon? No, Daniel didn't know anything about the cosmic conflict until it was already over and the angel told him about it. God's way of dealing with the situation was to send the archangel Michael, not a trained believer, to provide deliverance (v. 13). The Bible makes no mention of any other territorial conflict in the realm of spiritual warfare.

Scripture implies that Satan's hordes are highly regimented (cf. Eph. 6:12), but nowhere does the Bible say that Satan has assigned them to every geopolitical unit. Nowhere does the Bible give an example of a believer confronting or rebuking geographical demons. Nowhere does God's Word say that we are to command demons to give up any territory. In fact, nothing in Scripture offers any instructions for territorial warfare. No self-styled "expert" in the practice can legitimately claim to have gained his knowledge or skills from the Bible.

God's plan for spiritual warfare is not confined to a few experts. It is not a mystery. It is not complex. Training camps are not necessary. God's plan is clearly revealed in His Word to all believers, namely, "Resist the devil and he will flee from you" (James 4:7). Do the champions of today's spiritual-warfare movement think it is too simplistic to trust that God's plan will work?

Will Satan have us for breakfast? Should we fear being made into toast? That's not the picture we get from Paul, who declared that God "*always* leads us in triumph in Christ, and manifests through us the sweet aroma of the knowledge of Him *in every place*" (2 Cor. 2:14).

In Romans 8:37–39, Paul also said:

> In all these things we overwhelmingly conquer
> through Him who loved us. For I am convinced that
> neither death, nor life, nor angels, nor principalities,
> nor things present, nor things to come, nor powers,

nor height, nor depth, nor any other created thing,
    will be able to separate us from the love of God,
    which is in Christ Jesus our Lord.

The Greek word for "principalities" refers to both good and
fallen angels in the New Testament, but in verse 38 it probably
refers to the latter. In Christ we are secure against demons. The
Greek words for "height" and "depth" are astronomical terms.
The former refers to the location of a star at its zenith and the
latter at its nadir. We are secure against *everything* in the celestial
realm, including demons. Now that's territorial security!

Although we enjoy security in Christ, Satan nevertheless will
attack the church. The risen Christ makes that clear in Revelation
2—3, which contain letters He dictated to seven churches in the
cities of Ephesus, Smyrna, Pergamum, Thyatira, Sardis,
Philadelphia, and Laodicea. They were historical churches, but
they are also prototypes of churches that exist in all periods of
church history. Each of them has unique characteristics that the
Lord speaks to.

What did the Lord say to them? Five of the letters contain
warnings; two do not. The churches at Smyrna and Philadelphia
apparently needed no warning, but the other five stood in need
of dire warnings. There is also a progression in the warnings.
The second warning is more severe than the first, and so on.
The last warning addresses an apostate church. All the churches
began with good intentions, but a spiritual decline led to spiritual bankruptcy.

When the Lord warned the churches, He never instructed
them to engage in territorial warfare. He never told them to
rebuke Satan or command demons. He never instructed them to
claim victory and initiate a confrontation with the powers of
darkness. His instruction was nothing like the hocus-pocus often
advocated by today's self-proclaimed spiritual-warfare experts.

What exactly did Christ say? Let's find out. In the process
we'll see not only how Satan infiltrates the church, but also how
the Lord instructs us to deal with Satan's attacks.

THE CHURCH AT EPHESUS

The Ephesian church had an extraordinary beginning. Its founder was no less than the apostle Paul, and its pastors were Apollos and Timothy. The church began as an island of purity in a sea of wretchedness. Its members had been so successful in reaching out and purifying parts of the city that they brought to a halt some of the most complex systems of false religion in existence at that time. It's not surprising, therefore, that Christ began His letter by commending them:

> I know your deeds and your toil and perseverance, and
> that you cannot tolerate evil men, and you put to the
> test those who call themselves apostles, and they are
> not, and you found them to be false; and you have per-
> severance and have endured for My name's sake, and
> have not grown weary. (Rev. 2:2–3)

Ephesus wasn't an easy place to live in. Right in the middle of it was the temple of Diana, one of the seven wonders of the ancient world. Scores of eunuchs, thousands of prostitute-priestesses, and many heralds and flute players created a hysterical arena of music, orgies, and drunkenness. Heracleitus, a famous Greek philosopher from Ephesus, said that the morals of the city were worse than questionable.

In spite of all that, the Lord used Paul's preaching to reach many for Christ. The believers worked hard and endured their difficult circumstances patiently. They hated sin and would not tolerate it in their midst. In verse 6, Christ said to them, "You hate the deeds of the Nicolaitans, which I also hate." Apparently the Nicolaitans followed the teaching of Nicolas—a man who espoused sexual immorality. Clement of Alexandria, an ancient writer, said they abandoned themselves to pleasure like goats. We can't be sure what the Nicolaitans believed, but we do know that they practiced licentious behavior.

The church also dealt with false teachers, for they "put to the test those who call themselves apostles" (v. 2). They had a biblical standard—a statement of faith—by which they measured all would-be authorities. They were doctrinally sound. In verse 3, John said they were serving in Christ's name. Their motive was to glorify Christ, which is the greatest motive for anything a Christian does (1 Cor. 10:31).

But the church had one fatal flaw. The Lord put it in this way: "I have this against you, that you have left your first love" (Rev. 2:4). Love died in the church at Ephesus. They sponsored ortho-doxy, but they did not have a fervent love for Christ. The people turned their hot hearts for cold orthodoxy. They carried out a bib-lical ministry without any passion.

That's a serious problem. Think of it in this way: Your husband comes home to you and says, "I don't love you anymore; but don't worry—nothing will change. I'll still earn a living and eat with you, and sleep with you, and drive with you, and father your children. It will all be the same. I'll still be your husband; it's just that I won't love you anymore." Devastating! How would you feel if your spouse said that to you? Would that kind of relationship be enough for you? Now try to imagine how the Lord would feel if you said, "Lord, I don't love You like I once did—that's gone. But I want You to know I'll still come to church; I'll still sing, give, and even believe the truth. I just don't love You, that's all." Probably not one of us would come right out and say that, but the Lord knows whether it's true.

What about you? Is your enthusiasm for Christ still there? Do you have the same love for Him that you used to have? I hope you find yourself loving Him more and more each day! But if you find yourself loving anything in this world—yourself, your family, leisure, money, or success—more than you love Christ, you have lost your first love. If you're serving Christ but not loving Him, you've missed the purpose of the Christian life.

How can you reclaim your first love? By remembering what your life with Christ was like before your love grew cold (v. 5). Remember the warmth, joy, and exhilaration that were yours with Him. Interwoven with that remembrance is the need for repen-tance. If the first reaction you have to Christ is anything less than a consummate desire to know and serve Him, you've lost your first love. If the first reaction you have to another believer is anything but brotherly affection, you've lost your first love. You need to repent.

The fruit of repentance is that you will do the first works once more (v. 5). If your service is cold and mechanical, don't go to a spiritual-warfare seminar, but go back to where you started. Get back on your knees, get back to reading the Bible, get back to witnessing, get back into the fellowship. Stay close to the fire!

THE CHURCH AT PERGAMUM

Pergamum was a tough city. It was the center of the worship of Zeus, the greatest of all the Greek deities. A huge altar to Zeus had been built in Pergamum in the shape of a throne. Some commentators believe that the throne of Satan mentioned in verse 13 is a reference to the altar of Zeus, the most famous altar in the world at that time.

Pergamum also had its own god—Asclepius. He was considered the god of healing and has always been associated with snakes. The caduceus, the twisted serpent symbol that represents the medical profession, comes from Greek mythology and represents the god Asclepius. In a temple dedicated to him, there was a school of medicine where nonpoisonous snakes crawled all over the floor. The ill would lay on the floor so the snakes could crawl on them. Wherever the snakes touched them, they would supposedly be healed.

In the midst of such paganism was a small group of believers whom Christ commended:

> I know where you dwell, where Satan's throne is; and
> you hold fast My name, and did not deny My faith even
> in the days of Antipas, My witness, My faithful one, who
> was killed among you, where Satan dwells. (v. 13)

The Lord was saying, "I know everything about you. I know you're active in ministry, even though it's a rough city to serve in.

I know you dwell where Satan's throne is. I know you hold fast to My name and have not denied the faith. Some of you have even been martyred, including your dear brother Antipas." Although the church had endured great difficulties, the Lord still had a few things against it:

> You have there some who hold the teaching of Balaam,
> who kept teaching Balak to put a stumbling block
> before the sons of Israel, to eat things sacrificed to
> idols and to commit acts of immorality. (v. 14)

Balaam had led the Israelites to intermarry with pagans and follow their idolatrous practices (Num. 24:10—25:13). The same kind of problem occurred in the church at Pergamum—the people were compromising with the world. I don't know if Christians were actually intermarrying with non-Christians, but the church at Pergamum had begun to court the world and indulge in worldly things.

The church also was making allowances for the teaching of the Nicolaitans. Once a church tolerates sin in its midst, its message might still sound the same, but worldly compromise will eat away at its foundation and spoil its testimony. That's why Paul wrote:

> Do not be bound together with unbelievers; for what
> partnership have righteousness and lawlessness, or what
> fellowship has light with darkness? Or what harmony
> has Christ with Belial, or what has a believer in com-
> mon with an unbeliever? ... Therefore, come out from
> their midst and be separate. (2 Cor. 6:14–15, 17)

It amazes me how eagerly today's church tries to mimic the world. If the world's view of the family, women, or homosexuals changes, the church accommodates that change. The church becomes materialistic because the world is materialistic. The church becomes preoccupied with entertainment because the world is preoccupied with entertainment. Today's church has a tendency to jump on every bandwagon the world parades by us, because Christians today are so eager to identify with the world. The church is not supposed to be some benevolent, nonthreatening agency whose primary goal is to achieve prestige, popularity, and intellectual acceptance. Contemporary Christians seem to think that if the world likes us, it will like our Savior. That is not the case (John 15:18).

Today's church wants to buy into the world, but Christ's command for the church is the opposite: "Do not love the world nor the things in the world. If anyone loves the world, the love of the Father is not in him" (1 John 2:15). Surrounded by paganism and immorality, the church at Pergamum was buying into the world. If ever there was a prime candidate for so-called territorial warfare, Pergamum would have been it because Satan dwelt there (Rev. 2:13). How would the advocates of today's spiritual-warfare movement respond to a city like Pergamum? Here's what one student of the "experts" did in his neighborhood:

> For the last 10 years I have lived in the black community in Los Angeles. My neighbors and I have common enemies. Spirits of despair, hopelessness, depression, discouragement and rejection torment this community....
>
> Several years ago my staff and I went on a prayer walk around our neighborhood. We stood in front of every house, rebuked Satan in Jesus' name and prayed for a revelation of Jesus in the life of each family.[4]

Is that how we are to win our neighborhoods? Did Christ instruct the Christians in Pergamum to walk the roads and say, "In the name of Jesus, I rebuke Satan"? Did He tell Christians there to command the demons of paganism and immorality to leave the city? Hardly.

The Bible makes it clear that we are to win our neighborhoods by presenting the gospel to the lost (Matt. 28:19–20). How is our presentation made credible? Not by commanding demons, but by holy living (1 Peter 2:12). That's why it was necessary for the church at Pergamum to repent (Rev. 2:16).

When Satan attacks the church, he starts very subtly by causing us to lose our first love. Then we begin to compromise with the world. As our love cools, it becomes easier to fall into the trap of the world's system. By not loving God, we are prone to love what's around us.

If you are courting the world, what is God's battle plan for you? Not confronting the powers of darkness, but obeying Christ's command to repent. If you really love God with all your heart, soul, mind, and strength, your desire—above all things—will be to maintain His honor.

THE CHURCH AT THYATIRA

The church at Pergamum may have married the world, but the church at Thyatira was celebrating its anniversary. Ephesus had lost its first love, Pergamum had compromised with the world, and Thyatira had opened the floodgate to sin. So Christ responded to Thyatira,

> I have this against you, that you tolerate the woman
> Jezebel, who calls herself a prophetess, and she teaches
> and leads My bond-servants astray so that they com-
> mit acts of immorality and eat things sacrificed to
> idols. (v. 20)

The church had retained a measure of love, service, and faith (v. 19); but a false teacher, symbolically named Jezebel, seduced the church into the idol worship of the day. Back then idolatry involved illicit sexual activity. Verse 24 indicates that this Jezebel and her followers adhered to "the deep things of Satan."

How is the church to deal with such people? Are we to cast demons out of them? A young man claimed that's how he found deliverance from sin. This is his testimony:

Reared in a Baptist church, I accepted Christ as
Saviour at the age of six. My father was a deacon and
my mother was active in all the ladies' work. I soon fell
into the trap of religiousness, marking my spiritual
growth by the length of my attendance-pin chain.... I
grew theologically solid and spiritually dead, knowing
the truth but failing to live it.

I came to the conclusion that Christianity was fine
for life after death but that I needed something else for
here and now. I skimmed Zen, the Bhagavad-Gita,
poetry, and philosophy in a search for principles to
guide my life. I never even considered searching the
Scriptures. Raised in a fundamentalist church, I
assumed I already knew it all.

I didn't! On April 13, 1972, God set me free! I
was in a men's prayer meeting, watching as a friend
was *being prayed for deliverance*. A spirit was named,
Malicious Temper, that I suddenly realized fitted me
precisely. I knelt by myself to pray, only to find another
personality taking me over so completely as to render
me incapable of independent action.

Men quickly surrounded me and, before the night
was over, I was delivered of demon spirits that had
controlled me for over fourteen years! Demons of
Sorcery, Homosexuality, Pride and Murder and others
named themselves and left, leaving me free.[5]

How can someone who says that Christianity is fine for life after
death but not for here and now be a genuine Christian? Yet this
man giving his testimony and the author who cited it both evidently assume he was a true believer, though in bondage to Satan.
As we have seen, however, no true believer is ever indwelt by
demons. This man's testimony evidences no sorrow for sin, no confession of sin, and no turning from sin. He attributes his newfound
freedom merely to the absence of demons. How did Christ deal
with those who were following the deep things of Satan? Not by

casting out demons. He simply commanded Jezebel and her followers to repent of their sins. He warned them if they didn't He would punish them with death (v. 23). The Lord does not tolerate sin; He judges it.

Fortunately, not everyone in the church followed Jezebel (v. 24). What was Christ's instruction to them? Did He tell them to cast the demons of sexual perversion out of Jezebel? Did He tell them to bind Satan? No, Christ required only that they hold fast to holy living (vv. 24–25). That's because He wants us to pursue holiness, not clash with demons.

It's tragic that today's church has relinquished God's standard for holiness. I am often asked, "Do you actually discipline people in your church?"—as if that were some strange practice. I respond that of course we do because that's what the Bible tells us the church is to do (Matt. 18:15–17). The people who ask me that often reply, "We don't dare do that because we might offend someone." Churches with that attitude end up compromising with the world, which opens the floodgate to sin and Satan.

THE CHURCH AT SARDIS

Christ had particularly strong words for this church: "I know your deeds, that you have a name that you are alive, but you are dead" (Rev. 3:1). Sardis was one of the greatest cities of the ancient world. Its most famous king was Croesus. He was so rich that it's still proverbial even today to speak of someone being as rich as Croesus. The city of Sardis was synonymous with wealth, but that city and its church eventually died and went out of existence.

Because it was a degenerate church, Christ said to it, "Wake up, and strengthen the things that remain, which were about to die" (v. 2). The people were either dead or ready to die. All they had left was form. In *The Rime of the Ancient Mariner* Samuel Coleridge wrote, "Corpses man the ship; dead men pull the oars; dead men hoist the sails; dead men steer the vessel." That's what it was like in this church: Things were functioning, but there was no spiritual life.

What can revive a dead church? Repentance (v. 3).

True repentance is frankly a foreign concept to many churches today. What has happened?

> Why is it that the fear of God is no longer regarded
> as essential and central to true Christian living? We
> have made God small and man great.... Martin
> Luther put his finger on the issue long ago when he
> told the great humanist scholar Erasmus, "Your God
> is too manlike."[6]

This insidious practice of making God small and man great characterizes much of today's spiritual-warfare movement. How? By drawing undue attention to demons instead of Christ. People who ought to fear God fear Satan instead and focus on the powers of darkness. The modern spiritual-warfare movement has diluted biblical teaching about God's sovereignty, our sufficiency in Christ, salvation, and sanctification. God's simple battle plan for spiritual warfare is this: Turn from sin and turn to Christ.

What about you? Are you following God's plan, or are you preoccupied with the powers of darkness? The Lord, not Satan, was obviously David's fascination, for he wrote:

> Ascribe to the LORD, O families of the peoples,
> ascribe to the LORD glory and strength. Ascribe to
> the LORD the glory of His name; bring an offering
> and come into His courts. Worship the LORD in holy
> attire; tremble before Him, all the earth. (Ps. 96:7–9)

Think honestly about how that applies to you. Have you ever been fascinated by the glory and majesty of our sovereign Lord? Have you ever been gripped by the splendor of His presence? Having an accurate understanding of His Word will help you know Him like that. It's the foundation that will prompt you to say:

The LORD is my rock and my fortress and my deliverer,
my God, my rock, in whom I take refuge; my shield
and the horn of my salvation, my stronghold. I call
upon the LORD, who is worthy to be praised, and I am
saved from my enemies. (18:2–3)

THE CHURCH AT LAODICEA

The church at Laodicea was the worst of the lot. It had turned
apostate. Christ said, "I know your deeds, that you are neither
cold nor hot; I wish that you were cold or hot" (Rev. 3:15). The
one who is cold is not hypocritical; he is just uninterested and
unconcerned about the gospel. The Lord would rather have
people be like that than be lukewarm. At least you know where
they stand.

Hypocrisy nauseates Christ, for He said, "Because you are
lukewarm, and neither hot nor cold, I will spit you out of My
mouth" (v. 16). Those who are cold Christ draws to Himself by
preaching to them through His messengers. Those who are
hot—believing, saved, redeemed—He embraces. But those who
are lukewarm He spews out of His mouth. The church at
Laodicea is the hypocritical, phony church—the church that is
no church.

You will find theological liberalism in the Laodicean-type
churches of today. It exists under the guise of Christianity, but
its followers deny the Bible, the deity of Jesus Christ, the resurrection, and other major tenets of the Christian faith. When
you ask them about their church, they don't say, "We are seeing God's Word prevail. We are seeing people redeemed."
Instead they say, "I am rich, and have become wealthy, and
have need of nothing" (v. 17). What are they saying? "Look at
us. We're successful! We've got a big organization and a lot of
money!"

There are huge churches around the world—large denomi-
nations and massive religious systems that fall into this category.

They have all the money and trappings, but they are apostate. They're pitifully unaware that they really "are wretched and miserable and poor and blind and naked" (v. 17).

What is the solution for such a church? Is it to say, "Demon of hypocrisy, I command you to leave"? Or, "Satan, I bind you and order you stop your activity"? No, Christ's response was in stark contrast to that:

> I advise you to buy from Me gold refined by fire so
> that you may become rich, and white garments so that
> you may clothe yourself, and that the shame of your
> nakedness will not be revealed; and eye salve to anoint
> your eyes so that you may see. (v. 18)

Our Lord was not referring to the physical items, but to their spiritual counterparts. First, Christ said that the church was poor. That's why it needed to buy gold from Christ. In the Bible gold often symbolizes divine righteousness. When you receive Christ by faith, God imputes Christ's righteousness to you (Rom. 3:22). You might have everything the world has to offer, but if you don't have Christ, you really have nothing. That's why Jesus said, "What will it profit a man if he gains the whole world and forfeits his soul?" (Matt. 16:26).

The church was not only poor but also naked. That's ironic because Laodicea was the center of a large clothing industry. Its people were fashion conscious to an extreme. Special garments made in the city of Laodicea were world famous. The Laodicean Christians undoubtedly flaunted their clothing, but in reality they were naked because they didn't have the pure garments of Christ.

Christ also said the church needed eye salve. In the city of Laodicea there was a medical school at a temple of Asclepius. It was famous for a pharmaceutical it made called *tephra Phyrgia*, a compound that was crushed into a fine grain and mixed with a small amount of water to use as an eye salve.

It's as if Christ were saying, "You may think you are the ophthamologists of the world with your *tephra Phyrgia*, but I say you are in fact blind. If you really want to see, forget your accomplishments and open your eyes to the Word of God." Only Christ, the Great Physician, can apply salve to blind spiritual eyes and make them see.

Christ's concluding words to the Laodicean church included a gospel invitation because it was a lost, hell-bound church. In Revelation 3:19 He rebukes, chastens, and punishes the church because He wants it to repent. What can we learn from this church relative to our study? Again, that God's battle plan is for us to turn from sin, not to deliver a tongue-lashing to the powers of darkness.

THE CHURCH AT PHILADELPHIA

Although any church can eventually descend into the pit of apostasy, there are preservatives. The first is evangelism, which characterized the church at Philadelphia, one of the two churches Christ wrote to whom He had only good things to say. "I know your deeds. Behold, I have put before you an open door which no one can shut, because you have a little power, and have kept My word, and have not denied My name" (Rev. 3:8).

In verse 9 Jesus said opposition to the church came from a "synagogue of Satan." That refers to unbelieving Jewish people who opposed the testimony of the gospel in the city. In spite of such persecution, Christ had set an open door before this church. An open door to what? Undoubtedly this speaks of their ability to reach aggressively into the community with the gospel of salvation.

Why did this church have an open door for evangelism? Did the believers stand in front of every house in the city and say, "Demon of Philadelphia, I command you to give up your territory"? No, they were effective because they had kept Christ's Word and had not denied His name. So Christ opened the door for them. When Christ opens the door, Satan can't stop it. As we present the gospel to the lost, Christ is able to make satanic opposition bow down at our feet (v. 9).

How can you be effective against the powers of darkness? Not by commanding demons or rebuking Satan. Only God can do that

(Jude v. 9). You can be effective by presenting the gospel to the lost. That's because the gospel is "the power of God for salvation to everyone who believes" (Rom. 1:16).

THE CHURCH AT SMYRNA

God preserves the church not only through evangelism, but also through persecution. That's what characterized the church at Smyrna. Notice that Satan was the source of their persecution, for Christ said:

> I know your tribulation and your poverty (but you are
> rich), and the blasphemy by those who say they are
> Jews and are not, but are a synagogue of Satan. Do
> not fear what you are about to suffer. Behold, the devil
> is about to cast some of you into prison, so that you
> will be tested, and you will have tribulation for ten
> days. (Rev. 2:9–10)

Persecution was a normal part of early church life. One historian explains:

> To become a Christian meant the great renunciation,
> the joining of a despised and persecuted sect, the
> swimming against the tide of popular prejudice, the
> coming under the ban of the [Roman] Empire, the
> possibility at any moment of imprisonment and death
> under its most fearful forms.... He that would follow
> Christ must count the cost, and be prepared to pay the
> same with his liberty and life.... The mere profession of
> Christianity was itself a crime.... For [many] the Name
> itself ... meant the rack, the blazing shirt of pitch, the
> lion, the panther, or in the case of maidens an infamy
> worse than death.[7]

In light of Satan's opposition, what were the believers to do? Command the demon of Smyrna to give up its territory so persecution would cease? Bind Satan? Such efforts would have flown in the face of God because He was using Satan's persecution as part of His providential plan for this church.

Certainly Christ could have commanded Satan to cease persecuting the church, but He chose not to. In His divine wisdom He granted Satan permission to carry out his activity and encouraged the believers to endure it patiently. Why? To preserve the church's purity. You won't identify with a persecuted church unless you are serious about your commitment to Christ.

What can we learn from the churches at Philadelphia and Smyrna? That God does what He pleases to accomplish His sovereign, wise, and good purposes. He purposed to open the door of evangelism for the church at Philadelphia and permit the fires of opposition to rain on the church at Smyrna. God blessed them both.

God is not calling us to verbally assault demons. He is not calling us to become skilled in the things of Satan. He is calling us to be faithful to Him, like the churches at Smyrna and Philadelphia were. Doing so will prevent us from falling into the trap of the other five churches. May God help us be on the alert for Satan's attacks and help us remember Christ's warnings.

THE BELIEVER'S DUTY

࿔

Advocates of today's spiritual-warfare movement claim that we as believers are to confront the powers of darkness. One pastor wrote of this confrontation he had with a demon:

> *Pastor:* Claiming my full authority over you through my union with the Lord Jesus Christ, I command you to reveal how you were able to gain control in this person's life. I hold the blood of Christ against you and command you to tell me.
>
> *Demon:* She is afraid. We made her afraid. She's full of fear.
>
> *Pastor:* Is that the ground you claim against this child of God? Are you able to torment and work this destruction in her life because of fear?
>
> *Demon:* Yes, she is afraid all the time, and we can work through her fear.

> This conversation is reproduced as nearly as I can
> recall it from memory and from notes taken during an
> aggressive confrontation against the powers of darkness
> troubling a believer's life.[1]

Does that kind of aggressive encounter represent what you and I should be doing in spiritual warfare? Are we to talk to demons like that and give them orders? Absolutely not! God's Word makes it clear that such confrontations have no warrant.

I'm not sure what people mean when they talk about "taking authority in Jesus' name." A study of the concept of authority (Gk. *exousia*) in the New Testament reveals that word often describes a special status belonging only to Jesus Christ and His apostles.

Christ had authority because of His divinity (Matt. 28:18; John 5:27), and the apostles had authority derived from Him because they were His special representatives (1 Thess. 2:6; 2 Cor. 13:10).

They were privileged with supernatural ability—including the power to expel demons and disease (Mark 6:7; Luke 9:1–2; 10:19)—so that those who heard them would realize they spoke on God's behalf (2 Cor. 12:12; Heb. 2:3–4).

No one today has authority over demons and disease like the apostles did. In fact, 2 Peter 2:10–11 and Jude verses 8–10 imply that believers are *below* demonic spirits on the "authority ladder" and need to implore the Lord when dealing with them.

So "taking authority" over demon spirits or negative circumstances is not a biblical concept. Our method of dealing with Satan is to *resist him, firm in our faith* (James 4:7; 1 Peter 5:8–9).

What exactly does the Bible say our duty is as soldiers of the cross? Simply this: to endure hardship, fight the good fight, and stand firm in battle. Let's look at each aspect of our marching orders.

ENDURE HARDSHIP

In 2 Timothy 2:3–4, Paul wrote:

> Suffer hardship with me, as a good soldier of Christ
> Jesus. No soldier in active service entangles himself in
> the affairs of everyday life, so that he may please the
> one who enlisted him as a soldier.

How ironic that Christianity is so often presented as an eraser of hardship. In reality, being a true disciple of Christ is costly. It means taking up the cross daily. It means living with sacrifice, persecution, and ridicule.

Some think they can live the Christian life apart from hardship, but they are only deceiving themselves. They are asleep on the firing line—and there's no more dangerous position to be in.

Enduring hardship characterizes the good soldier who is on the front line "in active service" (v. 4). Such a soldier does not become wrapped in the nonessentials of this life.

Luke 9 gives three examples of people who would not follow Christ because they became entangled in the affairs of this life. The first individual said to Christ, "I will follow You wherever You go" (v. 57). Christ replied, "The foxes have holes and the birds of the air have nests, but the Son of Man has nowhere to lay His head" (v. 58). That individual was concerned about his personal comfort.

Christ said to another, "Follow Me" (v. 59). But he responded, "Permit me first to go and bury my father." That individual wanted his inheritance first. Christ replied, "Allow the dead to bury their own dead; but as for you, go and proclaim everywhere the kingdom of God" (v. 60). The text gives no indication that the person got Christ's message.

The third individual said, "I will follow You, Lord; but first permit me to say good-bye to those at home" (v. 61). He was unwilling to give himself wholeheartedly to Christ as Lord. Christ replied, "No one, after putting his hand to the plow and looking back, is fit for the kingdom of God" (v. 62).

Christ offered three individuals an opportunity to leave all and follow Him. But they were unwilling to do so. What about you? Are you willing to follow Christ? Or have you allowed the things of the world to entrap you?

How can you be a good soldier? Not by picking fights with demons. You will be a good soldier by severing yourself from the ties of the world.

Rather than being preoccupied with earthly affairs, the believer is to "please the one who enlisted him as a soldier" (2 Tim. 2:4). That refers to Christ, the believer's Commander in Chief. It's obvious Paul's desire was to please Christ, for he was willing to die for Him at any time if necessary (Acts 20:24). He was utterly devoted to Christ, and we should be as well.

After commanding us to suffer hardship as good soldiers, Paul continued, "Remember Jesus Christ, risen from the dead, descendant of David" (2 Tim. 2:8). The resurrection pictures God's destruction of death, which is Satan's greatest weapon. It also pictures salvation, for Christ's death was a sacrifice for sin. His being alive means the penalty for sin is satisfied.

The implication is that we are also to remember Christ's suffering. Hebrews 12:2 says that Christ endured the cross and despised the shame before sitting down at the right hand of God's throne. He was humiliated before He was exalted. Since suffering was the path the perfect Son of God followed, it's the path we should expect to follow as well (John 15:20).

It is popular in many circles today to preach a different message. Some have actually turned the gospel into a promise of prosperity. They promote the notion that God desires all believers to be healthy and wealthy. An unhealthy preoccupation with Satan and demons goes hand in hand with that unbiblical theology:

> The presence of demonic activity in the lives of
> Christians is an important plank in the prosperity
> platform. It is assumed that manifestation of demonic
> opposition today is the same as it was in the first cen-
> tury AD. The tendency is to attribute anything out of
> the ordinary or not readily explainable to the influ-
> ence of demons.
>
> The Hunters [Charles and Frances] provide a
> case in point: "When a doctor says there is no cure,

our spiritual antennas pick up the fact that it is a
spirit." They have concluded that all incurable diseases are caused by evil spirits. Demons inhabit not
only people, but also homes, cars, and other mechanical devices. This produces great consternation for
the believer who wants to experience blessings promised to him.

The process of casting out demons solves the
believer's "demonic dilemma." ... In the procedure for
casting out demons Satan is bound by the authority of
Jesus so that he cannot render aid to his evil associates.
Then the demon is addressed, commanded to name
himself and cast out. Since demons can do such things
as planting seeds of disease and stopping the flow of
financial wealth, the casting out of demons is necessary
to ensure continued health and prosperity.... Without
question the prosperity movement is characterized by
an obsession with the demonic.... [It] seems to have
reverted to a form of animism, which holds that evil
spirits inhabit and control both animate and inanimate
objects. Faith healers in the movement have more in
common with witch doctors than medical doctors.[2]

The prosperity message is a false gospel.[3] It contradicts the biblical meaning of discipleship, for Christ declared, "If anyone wishes
to come after Me, he must deny himself, and take up his cross and
follow Me" (Matt. 16:24). Hebrews 12:3 points us to the example
of Christ: "Consider Him who has endured such hostility by sinners against Himself, so that you will not grow weary and lose
heart." Following Him will help you endure hardship.

Another example to follow is the apostle Paul. He certainly
knew what enduring hardship was all about. Shut up in a filthy dun-
geon he wrote:

I suffer hardship even to imprisonment as a criminal; but
the word of God is not imprisoned. For this reason I

> endure all things for the sake of those who are chosen,
> so that they also may obtain the salvation which is in
> Christ Jesus and with it eternal glory. (2 Tim. 2:9–10)

Paul was considered a criminal and treated like one. When he wrote his second letter to Timothy, he probably was in the Mamertine prison in Rome. It was a pit without normal sanitation and jammed with people awaiting execution.

How did Paul respond to his imprisonment? Did he say, "Satan, I rebuke you and command you to set me free"? Did he bind the demon of Rome? No, his attitude was opposite to that. His awareness of God's sovereignty helped him to endure adversity. His life reflected the conviction that God was causing all things—even including imprisonment—for his ultimate good (Rom. 8:28). He knew that no one could incarcerate God's Word and that death would usher him into Christ's presence.

Seek to imitate Paul's attitude, and be willing to endure affliction for the sake of Christ. The motivation for doing so is God's promise that you will reign with the Savior in glory (2 Tim. 2:12). Until then, trust God to supply you with all the divine strength and power you need (2 Peter 1:3).

FIGHT THE GOOD FIGHT

Now that we're motivated to serve Christ regardless of the cost, what next? Paul said, "Fight the good fight, keeping faith and a good conscience" (1 Tim. 1:18–19). Now in fighting this fight, note that Paul doesn't specify that we're to speak to, command, or cast out demons. God's plan for spiritual warfare has nothing to do with exorcism, incantations, mantras, or mysticism. Fighting the good fight simply means that we are to keep the faith (uphold sound doctrine) and a good conscience (live holy lives).

Paul concluded his letter with a similar charge: "Fight the good fight of faith" (6:12). The Greek word translated "fight" (*agōni-zomai*, from which we get the English word *agonize*) implies that we are to struggle continually to uphold the truth of Scripture. It

was used in both military and athletic contexts to describe the con-
centration, effort, and discipline needed to win. All those qualities
are required for our battle against Satan and his cohorts as they
infiltrate the church and the world with their lies. But beware: Our
enemies fight dirty, "disguising themselves as apostles of Christ. No
wonder, for even Satan disguises himself as an angel of light.
Therefore it is not surprising if his servants also disguise themselves
as servants of righteousness" (2 Cor. 11:13–15).

Paul knew how to fight that kind of enemy. William
Hendriksen described Paul's perpetual warfare this way:

> It had been a fight against Satan; against the principali-
> ties and powers, the world-rulers of this darkness in the
> heavenlies; against Jewish and pagan vice and violence;
> against Judaism among the Galatians; against fanati-
> cism among the Thessalonians; against contention,
> fornication, and litigation among the Corinthians;
> against incipient Gnosticism among the Ephesians and
> Colossians; against fightings without and fears within;
> and last but not least, against the law of sin and death
> operating within his own heart.[4]

Paul spoke of the wounds he received in serving Christ: "I bear
on my body the brand-marks of Jesus" (Gal. 6:17). Those wounds
were a testimony of Paul's willingness to fight the good fight. His
attitude reminds me of Robert Browning's "Incident of the French
Camp." The poem tells of a young soldier who hurriedly came
from the battlefield to report victory to Emperor Napoleon. He
was so exhilarated to report the good news and so honored to be
chosen as the messenger that he was oblivious to his own severe
wounds. Napoleon, upon noting them, exclaimed:

> "You're wounded!" "Nay," the soldier's pride
>   Touched to the quick he said:
> "I'm killed Sire!" And his chief beside
>   Smiling the boy fell dead.

Upholding the revealed truth of God's Word will inevitably lead to conflict because many oppose the truth. But if you and I live in the light of eternity, that won't be an obstacle. An effort we exert in this short life for Christ's sake will be recompensed immeasurably in eternity. That's one reason Paul called it "the *good* fight" (1 Tim. 1:18).

J. C. Ryle comments further:

> Let us settle it in our minds that the Christian fight is a good fight—really good, truly good, emphatically good. We see only part of it yet. We see the struggle, but not the end; we see the campaign, but not the reward; we see the cross, but not the crown. We see a few humble, broken-spirited, penitent, praying people, enduring hardships and despised by the world; but we see not the hand of God over them, the face of God smiling on them, the kingdom of glory prepared for them. These things are yet to be revealed. Let us not judge by appearances. There are more good things about the Christian warfare than we see.[5]

What about you? Are you fighting the good fight? Are you contending for the faith (Jude v. 3)? Is it your desire to obey and proclaim the truth, no matter what the cost?

STAND FIRM

When I was in Scotland, a man approached me in Frazerborough and asked, "Is your father named Jack MacArthur?"

I told him yes.

He said, "Your father came to Ireland at least thirty years ago with two other men to hold a revival in Belfast and all around Ireland. I went to hear your father speak, and at the meeting I received Jesus Christ and dedicated my life to the ministry. I am a pastor because the Lord used your father to minister to me. Would you tell him that when you see him?"

I told him I would.

Then he asked, "Where is your father now?"

I told him he was ministering like he always had.

He asked, "Is he still faithful to the Word?"

I said, "Yes, he is still faithful—still standing."

"Good," he replied. "What happened to the other men?" I said, "I'm sorry to report that one became an apostate and the other died an alcoholic."

Three men went to Ireland and ministered to many people. But thirty years later, when the dust cleared, only one was left standing.

In 1 Corinthians 10:12, Paul said, "Let him who thinks he stands take heed that he does not fall." Satan doesn't want us to stand. That's why Peter warned:

> Be of sober spirit, be on the alert. Your adversary, the
> devil, prowls around like a roaring lion, seeking some-
> one to devour. But resist him, firm in your faith,
> knowing that the same experiences of suffering are
> being accomplished by your brethren who are in the
> world. (1 Peter 5:8–9)

We need to take this matter with the Devil seriously by being wide awake and spiritually alert. Our thinking must not be imbalanced, cluttered, confused, or self-centered. That's because Satan, our adversary, wants to capture us in sin. In his attempt to make us fall, he preys on us like a lion. Did you know that a lion tends to roar only when he already has his prey? Otherwise the prey would be forewarned of his approach. It is when the lion has cornered or killed his prey that he roars in triumph before devouring it.

Because Satan prowls like a lion, we are commanded to resist him (v. 9). The Greek word translated "resist" is a military term that speaks of taking a firm stand against an enemy. We are to stand against our hellish foe by being firm in the faith (v. 9). That speaks of purity in both doctrine and conduct. Do you want to be firm in the faith? Shun evil and draw near to God. When Satan or fleshly desires tempt you, resist. If we do that, Scripture guarantees that the Devil will flee (James 4:7).

Resisting the Devil is not a matter of speaking to him or rebuking him. Scripture clearly describes the armor we are to use in battle, and it consists of divine provisions we are to rely on. In Ephesians 6:11 and 13, Paul puts it in this way: "Put on the full armor of God, so that you will be able to stand firm against the schemes of the devil.... Take up the full armor of God, so that you will be able to resist in the evil day, and having done everything, to stand firm." "Full armor" means every piece issued is essential:

> If you are to be a soldier in this army, if you are to fight
> victoriously in this crusade, you have to put on the
> entire equipment given to you. That is a rule in any
> army.... And that is infinitely more true in this spiritual
> realm and warfare with which we are concerned ...
> because your understanding is inadequate. It is God
> alone who knows your enemy, and He knows exactly the
> provision that is essential to you if you are to continue
> standing. Every single part and portion of this armour is
> absolutely essential; and the first thing you have to learn
> is that you are not in a position to pick and choose.[6]

In verses 14–17 is a list of the combat equipment that the Holy Spirit issues to every believer at the moment of salvation:

1. The belt of truthfulness
2. The breastplate of righteousness
3. The shoes of the gospel of peace
4. The shield of faith
5. The helmet of salvation
6. The sword of the Spirit

This spiritual weaponry is not man made, for Paul wrote:

> Though we walk in the flesh, we do not war according
> to the flesh, for the weapons of our warfare are not of

the flesh, but divinely powerful for the destruction of
fortresses. We are destroying speculations and every
lofty thing raised up against the knowledge of God,
and we are taking every thought captive to the obedience of Christ. (2 Cor. 10:3–5)

"Weapons" refers to instruments of war. But these weapons are
special. They are not designed or manufactured by human intellect
or ingenuity. Neither are they mystical weapons. They are divine
weapons, effective at tearing down Satan's massive strongholds—
incredibly effective—for the verses picture an army moving against
a city and tearing down everything in its path.

Our spiritual weapons can be summed up in one word: obedience. Obedience comes by having our minds controlled by the
truth of God's Word. By obeying God's Word, you will stand firm
"in the evil day" (Eph. 6:13). When is the evil day? Every day has
been the evil day since Satan usurped the throne of the world. And
it will continue to be that way until he is cast into the bottomless pit.

The more we stand for Christ in the world, the hotter the battle will become. But if we are willing to endure hardship, fight the
good fight, and stand firm in battle, I believe God will give us joy
beyond anything we have ever known. That's because the greatest
joys come from the greatest victories.

HOW TO LIVE THE VICTORIOUS LIFE

In 2 Chronicles 20:15, the Spirit of the Lord said, "The battle is
not yours but God's." That verse is the motto for one variety of the
so-called deeper-life teaching called quietism. Quietists believe the
only way to live the Christian life is through passive surrender
rather than self-discipline. Their concept of Christian living is
reflected in the popular clichés "Let go and let God" and "I can't;
He can." Instead of struggling and striving, they say believers must
"surrender," taking no active role in the sanctification process.

At the other end of the spectrum is pietism. Pietists emphasize
self-discipline and holy living often to the extreme of adopting

legalistic standards for living. Pietism places so much emphasis on external righteousness and human effort that it ignores God's role in sanctification. The Pharisees were early advocates of a brand of pietism.[7]

Is there a balance somewhere between the two extremes? I believe so. On the one hand, we must depend on God—depend on His energy, power, and resources. On the other hand, we must obey God. That requires commitment and self-control.

The balance between God's effort and our effort is taught throughout Scripture. For example, Peter wrote:

> His divine power has granted to us everything per-
> taining to life and godliness, through the true
> knowledge of Him who called us by His own glory
> and excellence. For by these He has granted to us His
> precious and magnificent promises, so that by them
> you may become partakers of the divine nature, hav-
> ing escaped the corruption that is in the world by
> lust. (2 Peter 1:3–4)

God has given us everything that pertains to life and godliness. We therefore have everything we need to live a godly life. We do not lack any resources.

Peter went on to say:

> For this very reason also, applying all diligence, in
> your faith supply moral excellence, and in your moral
> excellence, knowledge, and in your knowledge, self-
> control, and in your self-control, perseverance, and
> in your perseverance, godliness, and in your godli-
> ness, brotherly kindness, and in your brotherly
> kindness, love. (vv. 5–7)

That is our part. We have all we need, but we do need to apply it.

That same balance is evident in Philippians 2:12–13. Paul wrote, "Work out your salvation with fear and trembling," then added "for it is God who is at work in you, both to will and to work for His good pleasure." In Colossians 1:29, Paul said, "I labor, striving according to His power, which mightily works within me." Both God and the believer work together. Spirituality is a joint effort.

The Bible teaches that we grow by being obedient to Christ. That includes our duty to endure hardship, fight the good fight, and stand firm in battle. Fulfilling that duty is not burdensome because God is able to "do far more abundantly beyond all that we ask or think, according to the power that works within us" (Eph. 3:20).

THE CALL
TO COMMITMENT

☙

Years ago President Theodore Roosevelt gave this penetrating call to commitment:

> It's not the critic who counts; not the man who
> points out how the strong man stumbled or where
> the doer of deeds could have done better. The credit
> belongs to the man who is actually in the arena,
> whose face is marred by dust and sweat and blood,
> who strives valiantly; who errs, and comes short again
> and again, because there is no effort without error
> and shortcoming; who does actually try to do the
> deed; who knows the great enthusiasm, the great
> devotion and spends himself in a worthy cause; who,
> at the worst, if he fails, at least fails while daring
> greatly. Far better is it to dare mighty things, to win
> glorious triumphs even though checked by failure,

than to rank with those poor spirits who neither
enjoy nor suffer much because they live in a gray twilight that knows neither victory nor defeat.[1]

The apostle Paul certainly didn't live in a gray twilight. He rec-
ognized that his battle was against a formidable Enemy—the very
Enemy who endeavored to withstand God in His own heavens and
who withstood man in his innocence in the garden of Eden. What's
more, this Enemy has tried on innumerable occasions to wipe out
the nation of Israel. He tried to stop the birth, life, and resurrection of Christ. Now he tries to destroy the church and hinder
service rendered by believers. In the future he will instigate worldwide rebellion against Christ both before and after the
establishment of the millennial kingdom.

If you don't recognize this Enemy, understand something of
his significance, and prepare for battle, you will lose out in life by
not fulfilling what God desires of you.

THE ENEMY'S STRATEGY

DOUBT

Satan tries to undermine God's character and credibility
because he wants you to doubt God. With that ploy he succeeded
in plunging the entire human race into sin. The crafty Serpent
questioned God's Word, saying to Eve, "Indeed, has God said
…?" (Gen. 3:1). He then impugned God's motives by saying that
God had a selfish, ulterior motive in forbidding Adam and Eve to
eat from the Tree of the Knowledge of Good and Evil (v. 5). He
was saying they couldn't trust God because He might say one
thing but mean another. Satan claims to be giving us the straight
scoop on life, but in reality it is Satan who is the liar (John 8:44).
God has no capacity to lie (Titus 1:2).

Satan wants you to doubt God—to doubt His Word and His
power. And we fall into his trap too often. We're tempted to worry
and lose control in a difficult situation because we don't really
believe God can solve our problem. Sometimes we doubt God's

grace, mercy, and forgiveness and therefore become burdened by feelings of anxiety and guilt. Some people wonder if God really loves them, especially when bad things happen, such as a spouse leaving or the death of a loved one.

How are we to deal with such doubt? Not by saying, "Demon of Doubt, I command you to come out." Not by saying, "In the name of Christ I rebuke Satan and command him to loosen his hold." Only Christ has that kind of power. We *are* responsible to resist doubt, as well as any other temptation, but we are not to dabble with demons. Dr. Peter Masters pointed out:

> Christians do have to engage in a great struggle against
> the wiles and temptations of the devil, but nowhere in
> the New Testament is temptation resisted by a process
> of commanding demons to loose their hold and leave a
> Christian's mind or body. Satan is resisted by being
> denied success in the temptation.[2]

Temptation operates this way: "Each one is tempted when he is carried away and enticed by his own lust. Then when lust has conceived, it gives birth to sin; and when sin is accomplished, it brings forth death" (James 1:14–15).

Do you realize that not every temptation comes from Satan? We can fall to temptation by yielding to our own flesh. And it's not necessary for you to know if the temptation is from Satan, a demon, or your own flesh. Why? Because the response is the same: Resist.

PERSECUTION

Satan uses not only doubt but also difficulties. He wants to make things hard, not easy, for the Christian. Often he uses persecution as his chief weapon. I remember a man telling me that he tried to talk to his brother about his newfound faith in Christ. As he showed his brother his Bible and began to talk about it, his brother grabbed the Bible and threw it across the room. He told him, "Don't you ever push that book on me!"

That is an illustration of rather mild persecution. Multitudes of
believers throughout church history were tortured and killed for
their faith. Satan uses all forms of persecution to attack Christians.

FALSE TEACHING

I often talk to people who have been Christians for a long time
yet understand very little of what the Bible says. One such individual didn't know what sanctification is. Others say, "What am I to
believe? I'm so confused." I believe the confusion is partly a ploy of
Satan to frustrate Christians. He does so by using teachers to present a plethora of contradictory doctrines and interpretations that
leave many baffled.

Why are there so many teachings over which Christians dis-
agree? One reason is many teachers arrive at what they believe is the
truth by intuition or a mystical experience. That practice has per-
meated today's spiritual-warfare movement. One man wrote this
about his experience as a young pastor:

> I often found myself crying out to God for revival dur-
> ing extended sessions of prayer. In the midst of one
> such prayer session an unusual, strong spiritual aware-
> ness suddenly overwhelmed me. I don't know how else
> to describe it. Although I did not hear a voice, there
> was a powerful communication to my spirit: *Before a
> revival like the one for which you are praying can come,
> there will have to be a strong encounter with Satan.*[3]

That pastor's experience may well have been sudden, unusual,
and strong, but he is wrong to assume it was spiritual. God com-
municates to us through His revealed Word, not through mystical
experiences. Too many people build belief systems on experiences
they have invented in their own minds. To seek such experiences
only opens one up to satanic influence or deception.

It is tragic that those in today's spiritual-warfare movement are
being drawn into the black hole of mystical experiences. What is the

remedy for such error? Careful exegesis and the systematic teaching of God's Word.

SELF-SUFFICIENCY

Satan wants us to believe we are self-sufficient and therefore urges us to trust in our own resources, rather than God. In the Old Testament he used that scheme against David:

> Satan stood up against Israel and moved David to number Israel. So David said to Joab and to the princes of the people, "Go, number Israel from Beersheba even to Dan, and bring me word that I may know their number." (1 Chron. 21:1–2)

David wanted to find out how strong he was, so he had his military adviser count the available soldiers. But God told him that was a terrible sin because his strength did not depend on the number of his troops, but on God. In Psalm 147:10–11, the psalmist said the Lord "does not delight in the strength of the horse; He does not take pleasure in the legs of a man. The LORD favors those who fear Him, those who wait for His lovingkindness." David's falling into . Satan's trap had serious consequences, for God sent judgment and 70,000 in Israel died.

It's easy for us to place our confidence in the wrong things. You might say, "I've memorized a book of the Bible. I've mastered some important principles. I've been to seminary. I'm ready and able to handle any problem that might come my way." But "let him who thinks he stands take heed that he does not fall" (1 Cor. 10:12). Your prayer life can easily become nonexistent and your devotions shallow. The Lord said, "Let not a wise man boast of his wisdom, and let not the mighty man boast of his might, let not a rich man boast of his riches; but let him who boasts boast of this, that he understands and knows Me, that I am the LORD who exercises lovingkindness, justice, and righteousness on earth; for I delight in these things" (Jer. 9:23–24).

We have seen that Satan tempts us with doubt, difficulties, false teaching, and self-sufficiency. That might leave you wondering, *How am I to deal with Satan's attacks? How am I to resist all his complex, subtle strategies?* The wonderful thing is that all his attacks can be dealt with in one simple way: by putting on the full armor of God (Eph. 6:13). Don't concentrate on what the Devil is doing, but on what you're to be doing. It doesn't matter that you know precisely when and how Satan is mapping every subtle scheme. We can't do that anyway. The only thing that does matter is that you put your armor on. If you do, you will be ready for battle.

READY FOR BATTLE

In Ephesians 6:14, Paul described the first piece of spiritual armor in this way: "Stand firm therefore, having girded your loins with truth." Let's call it the belt of truth since it is a reference to preparation, readiness, and commitment.

When the Israelites were called by God to leave for the Promised Land, they were told to have their loins girded in readiness. That was a common phrase for someone prepared to take a journey. When the Lord talked about His second coming, He said, "Let your loins be girded about, and your lights burning" (Luke 12:35 KJV). That refers to being ready to go at a moment's notice.

In Paul's day soldiers wore a tunic, which was a large square piece of material that had holes for the head and arms. It hung low and loose, so the soldier cinched it around his waist with a belt. When he was ready to fight, he would pull the four corners of his tunic up through the belt. That was known as girding one's loins. It gave the soldier the mobility and flexibility he needed for hand-to-hand combat.

It was also common for a Roman soldier to wear a strap. It was connected to the front of the belt, went over the soldier's shoulder, and connected to the belt in the back. He would attach his sword to the strap along with decorations or medals from battle. When a Roman soldier put on his belt, attached the strap, and hooked on his sword, he was ready to fight.

In the spiritual realm the Christian is to gird his or her loins "with truth" (Eph. 6:14). That can refer to either the content of truth (i.e., Scripture) or an attitude of truthfulness, sincerity, honesty, and integrity. Since Paul referred to Scripture as a spiritual weapon in verse 17, it seems he was referring to a Christian's attitude. The believer who girds his or her loins with truth has a heart for the battle because he or she is committed to Christ and His cause.

An attitude of commitment is foundational to victory. Zonik Shaham, a general in the Israeli armed forces, knows that to be true. After listening to me preach on this topic, he said to me, "I appreciated what you said about commitment because that is the whole issue with us. People think Israelis are a superpeople with superior intellect and strength. They think we win because of that, but we win by commitment. We still use the phrase 'gird up your loins' to mean commitment and preparedness.

"Let me give you an illustration of that. I have a Jewish friend who lives in the San Fernando Valley [in California]. His son desired to live in Israel. After living there for several years, he reached the age where he would have to enter the military or return to the United States. I thought that, like other Americans, he would choose the life of ease and return to America rather than enter the Israeli Army. So I was surprised when he joined the army.

"I then received a letter from him asking for a private appointment with me. I assumed he would ask me to find him a desk job. He showed up at my office requesting a favor. He told me that his assignment in the army was too easy. Instead, he wanted to be in the finest, most strategic, diligent, and difficult regiment in all the Israeli Army."

General Shaham informed him that a frontline, crack regiment of paratroopers has the most precarious duty. They drop into enemy territory before anyone else. Then he told him that the effort it takes to be in that regiment is incredible. The training closes with four days of relentless marching through the desert with a full pack to eventually climb the mountain that leads to the ancient fort of Masada. But that's what the man wanted, so he signed up.

General Shaham concluded, "That's why we win—we have people like him who are committed."

Unfortunately, many Christians lose battles because they are apathetic and uncommitted. They neglect to gird themselves properly.

SACRIFICIAL LIVING

How radical is the commitment our Lord calls for? It is utter and complete sacrifice of oneself. Paul wrote:

> Therefore I urge you, brethren, by the mercies of God, to present your bodies a living and holy sacrifice, acceptable to God, which is your spiritual service of worship. And do not be conformed to this world, but be transformed by the renewing of your mind, so that you may prove what the will of God is, that which is good and acceptable and perfect. (Rom. 12:1–2)

What does it mean to be a living sacrifice? It is a wholehearted surrender of one's body to spiritual service. That speaks of a determination to be useful to God. If you are not effectively ministering in some capacity, you have not truly given yourself as a living sacrifice. Service to God is the natural progression of commitment to Christ.

Many people claim to have committed their lives to Christ but offer no meaningful evidence. For example, I received this letter:

> Please meet with me and pray with me. I've driven my wife away because I taught her by example how to be a Sunday saint yet live any way you want all week long. And then when things started to fall apart in our marriage, and I tried to call us to prayer and Bible reading, she thought it was another one of my facades. I have outwardly lived as a Christian and have been active in the church, but the rest of the time I lived a lie.

Fortunately that man realized what he was doing. The believer who truly presents himself or herself as a living sacrifice will follow Christ without hypocrisy, no matter what the cost.

The sacrifice is to be not only living but also holy. The Greek word for "holy" means "set apart." That speaks of purity and freedom from sin. In Romans 6:13, Paul said, "Do not go on presenting the members of your body to sin as instruments of unrighteousness; but present yourselves to God as those alive from the dead, and your members as instruments of righteousness to God."

Instead of being set apart to God, many so-called Christians have become too comfortable in our society. They're willing to serve the Lord in their own way, but not if it costs them too much time or energy or if it conflicts with a favorite television program. They prefer to indulge in worldly pleasures to please themselves rather than give of themselves to please the Lord. Saint Augustine wrote, "Two cities have been formed by two loves; the earthly by the love of self, even to the contempt of God, the heavenly by the love of God, even to the contempt of self. The former, in a word, glories in itself, the latter in the Lord."[4] Many, sad to say, reside in the earthly city of self-love.

God doesn't want self-centered, halfhearted devotion. As we discovered earlier in our study of Revelation, He'd rather have us cold than lukewarm (3:15–16). He wants us to offer ourselves to Him completely. Why should we? Because of how merciful He has been to us (Rom. 12:1). He has freed us from sin, redeemed us in Christ, adopted us into His family, and granted us His divine power and the hope of heaven.

Yielding ourselves to God requires that we "not be conformed to this world" (Rom. 12:2). Think of the world as the floating mass of thoughts, opinions, hopes, and aims at any time current in the world. The world is Satan's instrument for promoting his goals and ambitions (1 John 5:19). To pattern yourself after it would be inconsistent with who you really are in Christ.

Instead you are to "be transformed by the renewing of your mind" (Rom. 12:2). The English word *metamorphosis* comes from the Greek word here translated "transformed." It speaks of a total change and involves a choice: to express your new nature through holy living or to allow your flesh to act unrighteously.

As you saturate your mind with God's Word, the Holy Spirit will take you from one level of glory to the next, conforming you to the image of Christ (2 Cor. 3:18). Only the believer with a spiritually transformed mind can resist the world, the flesh, and the Devil.

God's battle plan is not complex. There's no need to attend a spiritual-warfare training camp. You need not learn a secret strategy or formula. God's plan is that you present yourself to Him as a living sacrifice. By doing so, you will live victoriously over Satan and his evil ways.

Techniques vs. Character

Unfortunately, many who see themselves as spiritual-warfare specialists imply that it is not enough to clothe oneself in the armor of Ephesians 6 and present oneself to God as a living sacrifice. They believe we must also learn certain formulas to speak to, confront, command, cast out, and verbally spar with evil spirits. If you're not practicing this kind of warfare, they imply, you're not really in the battle. They believe dealing with demonic power is a highly dangerous thing for Christians who have not learned the proper techniques. Spiritual warfare has thus become more a matter of learned skill than spiritual character.

The lore of the modern spiritual-warfare movement is filled with accounts like this:

> Janelle was a Christian woman with severe emotional problems who was brought to me by her elderly pastor. Janelle's fiancé, Curt, came with them....
>
> I said, "Janelle, we can help you with your problems because there is a battle going on for your mind which God has given us authority to win." As soon as I spoke those words Janelle suddenly went catatonic. She sat still as a stone, eyes glazed over and staring into space....

"Well, there's nothing to worry about. I've seen it before," I said. "We're going to take authority over it, but it's important that you two [Curt and the pastor] affirm your right standing with God in order to prevent any transference of this demonic influence." ...

When I turned to lead Curt in prayer, he started to shake.... He began confessing sin in his life, including the revelation that he and Janelle had been sleeping together.... All the while Janelle sat motionless, totally blanked out.

After we had prayed together about getting his life straight with God, I gave Curt a sheet of paper with a prayer on it to read. As soon as Curt began to read the prayer, Janelle snapped to life. She let out a menacing growl, then lashed out and slapped the paper out of Curt's hands.... I addressed the demonic influence in Janelle: "In the name of Christ and by His authority, I bind you to that chair and I command you to sit there." ...

Then I prayed, "Lord, we declare our dependence on You, for apart from Christ we can do nothing. Now, in the name and authority of the Lord Jesus Christ, we command Satan and his forces to release Janelle and to remain bound within her so she will be free to obey God and her Heavenly Father." Suddenly Janelle snapped out of her catatonic state.

"Do you remember anything we've done here?" I asked her.

"No, what happened?" she responded with a puzzled expression.

"It's nothing to worry about," I told her. "Somehow Satan has gained a foothold in your life. But we would like to walk you through the steps to freedom in Christ." About an hour later Janelle was free....

Once Janelle renounced her involvement with sin and Satan, his hold on her was canceled, and he had to leave.[5]

What about that encounter? Besides the author's claim to an authority he does not possess,[6] it raises serious questions about the nature of salvation. Can we assume Janelle was a genuine believer? Can a person who hasn't previously renounced sin and Satan be truly converted? As we noted before, the indwelling of a demon evidences the absence of genuine salvation. Because the advocates of today's spiritual-warfare movement have a shallow and fuzzy view of the true meaning of salvation, they are quick to accept a person's profession, even if there is no evidence of any commitment to Christ.

Charles Spurgeon wrote:

> If the man does not live differently from what he did
> before, both at home and abroad, his repentance needs
> to be repented of, and his conversion is a fiction. Not
> only action and language, but spirit and temper must
> be changed.... Abiding under the power of any known
> sin is a mark of our being the servants of sin, for "his
> servants ye are to whom ye obey."[7]

A shallow view of salvation depreciates the doctrine of sanctification. When God saves someone, He promises to conform that person to Christ's image (Rom. 8:29; Phil. 1:6). Thomas Watson defined sanctification in this way:

> It is a principle of grace savingly wrought, whereby the
> heart becomes holy, and is made after God's own
> heart. A sanctified person bears not only God's name,
> but His image....
>
> Sanctification is our purest complexion, it makes us
> as the heaven, bespangled with stars; it is our nobility,
> by it we are born of God, and partake of the divine
> nature; it is our riches, therefore compared to rows of
> jewels, and chains of gold....
>
> It is our best certificate for heaven. What evidence
> have we else to show? Have we knowledge? So has the

devil. Do we profess religion? Satan often appears in
Samuel's mantel, and transforms himself into an angel
of light.... Sanctification is the firstfruits of the Spirit;
the only coin that will pass current in the other world.[8]

Advocates of the modern spiritual-warfare movement believe
they have the ability to command Satan and all his forces. But as we
have seen, no created being has that ability, not even the archangel
Michael (Jude v. 9). Those who think they have that kind of power
are deceived. The whole approach reflects an exaltation of self and
a depreciation of Christ's salvation. In Christ we have *instantaneous*
deliverance from Satan (Col. 1:13). It doesn't take an hour of
indoctrination or the constant haranguing of demons.

This formulaic approach to confronting demons cannot be found
in any of the New Testament instructions to Christians. If such
means are essential to confront the powers of darkness, why did the
Holy Spirit omit that information from Ephesians 6? Why among all
the biblical admonitions to Christians are there no instructions like.
those detailed in the plethora of spiritual-warfare guides being published today? If Christians really must learn techniques for casting out
demons, why doesn't Scripture spell them out?

The reason is that spiritual warfare is *not* a matter of technique,
but of spiritual character. The emphasis of nearly all apostolic teaching underscores this. Read the New Testament epistles. You will
not find the fixation with demonic powers that characterizes much
of the church today. In fact, you will find nothing instructing
Christians to seek out, speak to, defy, deride, or cast out demons.

THE PURSUIT OF EXCELLENCE

What you *will* find are admonitions to put aside sin and put on spiritual virtues. Peter wrote, "Applying all diligence, in your faith
supply moral excellence, and in your moral excellence, knowledge,
and in your knowledge, self-control, and in your self-control, perseverance, and in your perseverance, godliness, and in your
godliness, brotherly kindness, and in your brotherly kindness, love"

(2 Peter 1:5–7). Then he added, "If these qualities are yours and are increasing, *they render you neither useless nor unfruitful* in the true knowledge of our Lord Jesus Christ" (v. 8).

We are to pursue spiritual excellence, not demons. Paul wrote, "This I pray, that your love may abound still more and more in real knowledge and all discernment, so that you may approve the things that are excellent, in order to be sincere and blameless until the day of Christ" (Phil. 1:9–10).

"Real knowledge" speaks of full or advanced knowledge. The apostle is not speaking of some mystical knowledge, but knowledge of God and of His Word. Did you realize that the divine love flowing through believers is regulated by an intimate understanding of God's Word? It is not an uncontrolled emotion; real love is anchored in convictions based on the revealed truths of Scripture. Our love is to abound in "all discernment." That speaks of moral perception, insight, and the practical application of knowledge.

Why are we to have this knowledge and discernment? To "approve the things that are excellent"—that speaks of the ability to make correct spiritual decisions. Knowledge and discernment are thus essential prerequisites to spiritual excellence. Pursuing these things is far more important to victory in spiritual warfare than pursuing an already defeated foe.

BUCKLING THE BELT OF TRUTH

And if our love abounds in knowledge and discernment, not only will we be able to approve things that are excellent—we will also "be sincere and blameless until the day of Christ" (v. 10). That brings us right back to the belt of truth. "Sincere" means "genuine." It refers to commitment and truthfulness—the very stuff the belt of truth is made of. Some think the Greek word originally pictured the sifting of grain; that is, a believer is to have the impurities of his life sifted out, so he or she can be pure.

Another ancient word picture is this:

In ancient times ... the finest pottery was thin. It had a
clear color, and it brought a high price. Fine pottery
was very fragile both before and after firing. And ...
this pottery would [often] crack in the oven. Cracked
pottery should have been thrown away. But dishonest
dealers were in the habit of filling in the cracks with a
hard pearly wax that would blend in with the color of
the pottery. This made the cracks practically unde-
tectable in the shops, especially when painted or
glazed; but the wax was immediately detectable if the
pottery was held up to light, especially to the sun. In
that case the cracks would show up darker. It was said
that the artificial element was detected by "suntesting."
Honest dealers marked their finer product by the cap-
tion sine cera—"without wax."[9]

Our lives must be free from the wax of hypocrisy. Our commitment must be genuine. Some in the church appear as fine pottery,
but they are not. Their lives have cracks filled with the wax of religious activity. When held up to the light of God's Word, the wax of
false profession becomes evident.

Many Christians mask their problems without ever dealing with
them. They never let anyone see who they really are. That prevents
a fellow believer from coming alongside to help them with God's
Word. If you hide behind respectability and spirituality, you are
playing into Satan's hands, for he wants you to cover up your sin.
Instead of giving the Devil an advantage, you should face your sin
and deal with it in a biblical manner. Be genuine before others, and
be willing to receive help.

What is God's battle plan? Saying, "Satan I bind you"? Those
are mere words. Rather, you need to put your armor on, and the
first piece is the belt of truth. If we live lives of sincere commitment
to Him, we will leave no room for Satan to gain an advantage on
the battlefield. What's more, God will be glorified in us.

PROTECTING OUR MINDS AND EMOTIONS

ॐ

John Bunyan, author of *The Pilgrim's Progress*, wrote another famous allegory called *The Holy War*. It begins:

> In this gallant country of Universe, there lies a pleasant and peaceful municipality called Mansoul. The picturesque architecture of this town, its convenient location, and its superior advantages cannot be equaled under heaven....
>
> Once upon a time, a mighty giant named Diabolus made an assault upon this famous town of Mansoul. He tried to take it and make it his own habitation. This giant was the terrible prince of darkness. He was originally one of the servants of King Shaddai, who had placed him in a very high and mighty position....
>
> Knowing they had lost their positions and the King's favor forever, Diabolus and his rebels turned their pride into hatred against Shaddai and his Son.

They roamed about in fury from place to place in
search of something that belonged to the King on
which to take their revenge.

At last they happened to find this spacious country
of Universe, and they steered their course toward the
famous town of Mansoul. Considering it to be one of
the chief works and delights of King Shaddai, they
decided to make an assault upon the town....

When they found the place, they shouted horribly
for joy and roared as a lion over its prey, saying: "Now
we have found the prize and how to take revenge on
King Shaddai for what he has done to us." So they
called a council of war and considered what methods
they should use to win this famous town of Mansoul
for themselves.[1]

Today Satan continues to assault the town of Mansoul. His
attacks center in two areas: the mind and the emotions. Satan wants
to snatch the Word of God from you and fill your mind with lies,
immorality, and false doctrine. He wants you to think that sin is not
so bad. He wants to drown you in a sea of sin so that you become
very tolerant of it. He wants to entertain you with sin so that you
won't think it's as evil as it really is. He wants you to laugh at sin
on television or at the movies. He wants to twist your thinking by
putting sinful ideas to appealing music. He wants to confuse your
emotions by corrupting your desires and drawing your affections to
the wrong things. He wants to destroy your conscience, so it will
no longer warn you. He wants to debilitate your will and get you
to do things you shouldn't do.

How are we to deal with Satan? The proponents of today's spiritual-warfare movement call for supernatural confrontations with
the powers of darkness—what they refer to as "power encounters."
One writer explained it in this way:

We must be prepared for a confrontation with spiritual
powers—a power encounter—and must in addition be

prepared to expose Satanic deception with the truth
and to demonstrate the power of God over the deceiving spirits, not simply to talk about it.[2]

He is speaking of rebuking demons with phrases such as "Satan,
I bind you," commanding them, and verbally casting them out. His
understanding of spiritual warfare is extrapolated from a few pas-
sages of Scripture that detail incidents in the ministry of Jesus, who
healed the sick and cast out demons.

Is Miracle Power Available Today?

That kind of reasoning reveals a misunderstanding of the primary
reason for Christ's miracles. They were not an example for us to
follow, but a unique demonstration that He was the promised
Messiah. They were His messianic credentials. That's how the
apostle John understood them:

> Therefore many other signs Jesus also performed in the
> presence of the disciples, which are not written in this
> book; but these have been written so that you may believe
> that Jesus is the Christ [the Messiah]. (John 20:30–31)

Jesus Himself said, "The works which the Father has given Me
to accomplish—the very works that I do—testify about Me, that
the Father has sent Me" (John 5:36).

When John the Baptist began to doubt whether Christ was the
Messiah, Christ told John's disciples to encourage him with these
words: "Go and report to John what you hear and see: the blind
receive sight and the lame walk, the lepers are cleansed and the deaf
hear, and the dead are raised up" (Matt. 11:4–5).

Those in today's spiritual-warfare movement not only fail to
acknowledge the primary purpose of Christ's miracles, but also fail
to achieve the Lord's results. Christ's healings were immediate and
restored complete health to the afflicted. His miracles were also

undeniable. Everyone, including His enemies, was amazed and unable to deny or discredit them (Matt. 9:1–8; John 9:1–41).

The results of the modern spiritual-warfare movement fall embarrassingly short of Christ's example. According to his own statistics, one advocate admitted:

> 71 percent of the people I have prayed for over the last
> two years are still sick to some degree after the prayer
> is over.... I don't think this is strange.... I have heard
> John Wimber [another advocate] say on occasion,
> "More people I pray for are not healed than are."[3]

If the proponents of today's spiritual-warfare movement were capable of following the Lord's example, they would be able to demonstrate undeniable, immediate, and absolute success in all cases of healing and demon possession.

Faced with that dilemma, some focus instead on the example of the apostles. They try to support their position from Luke 9:1, which says that Christ "called the twelve together, and gave them power and authority over all the demons and to heal diseases."

In Matthew 10:5–10, a parallel passage, Christ said to the twelve apostles:

> Do not go in the way of the Gentiles, and do not enter
> any city of the Samaritans; but rather go to the lost
> sheep of the house of Israel. And as you go, preach,
> saying, "The kingdom of heaven is at hand." Heal the
> sick, raise the dead, cleanse the lepers, cast out demons.
> Freely you received, freely give. Do not acquire gold, or
> silver, or copper for your money belts, or a bag for your
> journey, or even two coats, or sandals, or a staff; for the
> worker is worthy of his support.

Does that mean every believer today is to do the same? No. Those miracles attested to the unique authority and ministry of the apostles. They were apostolic credentials. The apostle Paul described them as "the signs of a true apostle" (2 Cor. 12:12). If all believers were expected to perform miracles, miracles could not have been a true sign of apostleship. That's because a sign has to be distinct to be helpful. The apostolic miracles were unique to the apostles.

Notice that Jesus told the Twelve to go exclusively to the Jewish people. Peter Masters has written,

> Jesus was, in effect, saying to the covenant people, "By these powerful signs, done in My name, you will know that the kingdom of God has come and a new age has dawned. Your promised Messiah has come!"
>
> In no way were these missions a pattern for the "normal" work of disciples, as we can tell from the very limited duties which they were assigned. Would the Lord wish us to restrict our mission to Jews? Does He forbid His missionaries today to accept payment or to possess a change of clothing? Does He command us to be entirely dependent upon local hospitality? ...
>
> The trouble is that the exorcists have developed a confrontational mentality.... Instead of seeing the spiritual warfare as it is presented in the Bible, where the devil is fought with the weapons of prayer, preaching, witness, godly living, obedience to Scripture and faith in the promises, these would-be exorcists want to engage in hand-to-hand combat, sensing, seeing and hearing the powers of darkness and striking them with dramatic words of authority.... Here the air is thick with concepts which change precariously between the superstitions of medieval Rome and the notions of Eastern, pagan religions.[4]

THE BREASTPLATE OF RIGHTEOUSNESS

When Satan assaults Mansoul—when he attacks our mind and emotions—what are we to do? Have a power encounter? No. As we are seeing, Scripture gives clear instructions: We are to arm ourselves with spiritual armor, including "the breastplate of righteousness" (Eph. 6:14). Roman soldiers had different types of breastplates. Some were made of heavy strips of linen that hung down very low. Pieces of metal or thin slices from the hooves and horns of an animal were hooked together and hung from the linen.

The most familiar type of breastplate was the molded metal chest plate that covered the vital areas of the torso from the base of the neck to the top of the thighs. The soldier needed to protect that area because in those days much of the fighting was with a short sword in hand-to-hand combat.

The breastplate covered two vital areas: the heart and the viscera, or what the Jewish people referred to as "the bowels." In Hebrew culture the heart symbolically represented the mind or the thinking process (e.g., Prov. 23:7). The bowels became a reference to the emotions because of the way our emotions can affect how our intestinal organs feel. The mind and emotions encompass everything that causes a person to act: his knowledge, understanding, conscience, will, desires, and drives.

God has provided the breastplate of righteousness to protect your mind and emotions. What is this righteousness specifically? There are three possibilities: our own righteousness, imputed righteousness, and practical righteousness.

SELF-RIGHTEOUSNESS?

Satan's ultimate goal is to destroy men and women, preventing them from becoming citizens of heaven. How does Satan attempt to achieve that goal? By having people believe they are going to heaven because of their good deeds. Christ addressed that very issue in Luke 18:10–13 with this parable:

> Two men went up into the temple to pray, one a
> Pharisee and the other a tax collector. The Pharisee
> stood and was praying this to himself: "God, I thank
> You that I am not like other people: swindlers, unjust,

adulterers, or even like this tax collector. I fast twice a
week; I pay tithes of all that I get."

But the tax collector, standing some distance away,
was even unwilling to lift up his eyes to heaven, but
was beating his breast, saying, "God, be merciful to
me, the sinner!"

The Pharisee was proud of himself, thinking, *I'm so good. I've
arrived*. In contrast, the tax collector was contrite, for he realized
his sinfulness in light of God's holiness. Christ said, "I tell you, this
man [the tax collector] went to his house justified rather than the
other; for everyone who exalts himself will be humbled, but he who
humbles himself will be exalted" (v. 14).

Who was righteous? The man who thought he could be righteous on his own or the man who knew he couldn't? You could title
the story "The good man who went to hell and the bad man who
went to heaven."

Don't be deluded by Satan. If you think you can merit your way
into heaven by living a good life, you are wearing the wrong breastplate. All your best efforts apart from God won't help. As Isaiah
said, "All our righteous deeds are like a filthy garment" (64:6).
That's the best we can offer to God.

If anyone could get into heaven by his or her own righteousness,
it would have been Paul. In Philippians 3:4, he said, "If anyone else
has a mind to put confidence in the flesh, I far more." Paul had
more going for him than anyone. He was "circumcised the eighth
day, of the nation of Israel, of the tribe of Benjamin, a Hebrew of
Hebrews; as to the Law, a Pharisee; as to zeal, a persecutor of the
church; as to the righteousness which is in the Law, found blameless" (vv. 5–6). If self-righteousness were the way into the kingdom,
he could lay claim to it. But he could not. No one can.

In Romans 3:10–12, Paul said this about humanity: "There is
none righteous, not even one; there is none who understands,
there is none who seeks for God; all have turned aside, together
they have become useless; there is none who does good, there is
not even one." The Greek word for "useless" speaks of going sour
like milk. The whole human race has gone sour. "All have sinned

and fall short of the glory of God" (v. 23). You will become a victim of the forces of hell if you try to protect yourself with your own righteousness.

IMPUTED RIGHTEOUSNESS?

Another possibility to consider is that the breastplate refers to imputed righteousness. That refers to God's clothing a person in the righteousness of Christ at the moment of salvation. It's what Paul described in pointing out the futility of self-righteousness:

> I count all things to be loss in view of the surpassing
> value of knowing Christ Jesus my Lord, for whom I
> have suffered the loss of all things, and count them but
> rubbish so that I may gain Christ, and may be found in
> Him, not having a righteousness of my own derived
> from the Law, but that which is through faith in
> Christ, the righteousness which comes from God on
> the basis of faith. (Phil. 3:8–9)

In effect Paul was saying, "To enter heaven I must have the righteousness of God that comes by faith in Christ." When you become a Christian, God covers you with the canopy of Christ's absolute holiness. From that moment throughout eternity, whenever God looks at you, He sees the righteousness of Christ. In 2 Corinthians 5:21, Paul put it in this way: "He made Him who knew no sin to be sin on our behalf, so that we might become the righteousness of God in Him." Only Christ can provide true deliverance from Satan. By clothing you with His righteousness, He keeps you from the Evil One (1 John 5:18). This famous hymn speaks of that great reality:

> Jesus, Thy blood and righteousness
> My beauty are, my glorious dress;
> 'Midst flaming worlds, in these arrayed,
> With joy shall I lift up my head.

Bold I shall stand in Thy great day,
For who aught to my charge shall lay?
Fully absolved through these I am,
From sin and fear, from guilt and shame.

PRACTICAL RIGHTEOUSNESS?

While imputed righteousness assures you of ultimate victory over Satan, practical righteousness enables you to win the daily skirmishes. What is practical righteousness? Living a holy life.

Paul's desire was for his practical righteousness to match his positional righteousness, for he wrote, "I press on toward the goal for the prize of the upward call of God in Christ Jesus" (Phil. 3:14). The Greek word translated "press on" pictures a sprinter and speaks of an aggressive, energetic endeavor. Paul was running with all his might, straining every spiritual muscle. What was he pursuing? To be like Christ.

Becoming like Christ requires a lifetime commitment with maximum effort. J. C. Ryle explained it in this way:

> It [true Christianity] admits no breathing time, no armistice, no truce. On weekdays as well as on Sundays, in private as well as in public, at home by the family fireside as well as abroad, in little things, like management of tongue and temper, as well as in great ones, like government of kingdoms, the Christian's warfare must unceasingly go on.
>
> The foe we have to do with keeps no holidays, never slumbers and never sleeps. So long as we have breath in our bodies we must keep on our armour and remember we are on an enemy's ground....
>
> Let us take care that our own personal religion is real, genuine and true. The saddest symptom about many so-called Christians is the utter absence of anything like conflict and fight in their Christianity. They eat, they drink, they dress, they work, they amuse

themselves, they get money, they spend money, they
go through a scanty round of formal religious services
once or twice every week. But of the great spiritual
warfare—its watchings and strugglings, its agonies and
anxieties, its battles and contests—of all this they
appear to know nothing at all. Let us take care that
this case is not our own.[5]

Dr. Ryle thus spoke of spiritual warfare as an inner struggle for
personal holiness. That is a far more biblical way to characterize the
Christian's warfare than those today who believe spiritual warfare is
basically a series of personal confrontations with demons.

Unfortunately, in all the fuss about spiritual warfare today, personal holiness is becoming a forgotten commodity. Instead of
pursuing holiness, many Christians are wearing paper armor. Too
many have substituted seminars, techniques, and methods for the
spiritual armor of Ephesians 6.

The techniques they espouse resemble the apparatus of the
occult. Read, for example, this list of definitions from a standard
dictionary:

> **Clairvoyance**: The power or faculty of discerning objects not
>   present to the senses.… [The] ability to perceive
>   matters beyond the range of ordinary perception.
> **Divination:** The art or practice that seeks to … discover
>   hidden knowledge.
> **Magic:** An extraordinary power or influence seemingly
>   from a supernatural source.
> **Medium:** An individual held to be a channel of communica-
>   tion between the earthly world and a world of spirits.
> **Wizardry:** A seemingly magical transforming power or
>   influence.[6]

Are those the kinds of things Christians are to be dabbling in? Do
self-proclaimed experts of spiritual warfare really know secret formulas and magic phrases for fighting the powers of darkness? If so, they

have one up on the apostle Paul: He obviously didn't know how to "bind" the Devil, because Satan hindered him (1 Thess. 2:18)!

Why such an unhealthy fascination with Satan and demons? Many are caught up in mysticism, imagination, or hysteria. As a result, they make themselves *more* vulnerable to demonic deception. Jesus said *many* will claim to cast out demons and perform other miracles in His name, only to be ultimately rebuffed by Him as false teachers (Matt. 7:21–23).

We dare not let *anything*—even sensational experiences with supernatural powers—divert us from the issue of personal holiness. That is where the real battle is most intense.

Why do we need to protect our thinking and emotions? Because Satan operates like a military commander. When a commander is about to engage in battle with another army, the first thing he does is send out an advance group. Their mission is to establish a beachhead. From there, infiltration into enemy lines takes place. Satan uses the same tactic against the believer, trying to find an area of weakness in the believer's armor. He will exploit whatever weakness he finds.

In his classic book *The Christian in Complete Armour*, Puritan minister William Gurnall offered this practical counsel on how to maintain holiness:

> Be sure to get some Christian friend whom thou mayst
> trust above others to be thy faithful monitor. O that
> man hath a great help for the maintaining the power of
> godliness, that has an open-hearted friend that dare
> speak his heart to him!
>
> A stander-by sees more sometimes, by a man, than
> the actor can do by himself, and is more fit to judge of
> his actions than he of his own. Sometimes self-love
> blinds us in our own cause, that we see not ourselves
> so bad as we are; and sometimes we are over-suspicious
> of the worst by ourselves, which makes us appear to
> ourselves worse than we are.
>
> Now that thou mayst not deprive thyself of so
> great help from thy friend, be sure to keep thy heart
> ready with meekness to receive, yea, with thankfulness

to embrace, a reproof from his mouth. Those that cannot bear plain dealing hurt themselves most; for by this
they seldom hear the truth.[7]

How are we to protect ourselves? By holy living, not by power
encounters. In Romans 13:12–14, Paul said it in this way:

> The night is almost gone, and the day is near.
> Therefore let us lay aside the deeds of darkness and put
> on the armor of light. Let us behave properly as in the
> day, not in carousing and drunkenness, not in sexual
> promiscuity and sensuality, not in strife and jealousy.
> But put on the Lord Jesus Christ, and make no provi-
> sion for the flesh in regard to its lusts.

The light signifies holiness and purity; darkness signifies evil.
Casting off the works of darkness and putting on the armor of light
are the same as putting on the breastplate of righteousness. Get rid
of any evil in your life, and enjoy a holy, righteous relationship with
the Lord. By protecting your mind and emotions, you will be
impregnable against Satan.

But without the breastplate of holy living you will become
unproductive, diminish your capacity for serving God, and bring
reproach to God's glory. The apostle John warned, "Watch out that
you do not lose what you have worked for, but that you may be
rewarded fully" (2 John v. 8 NIV). Keep your breastplate in place!

THE GOOD NEWS
OF PEACE

When I was playing football in college, one of our games took place at the Rose Bowl. Before the game I had to choose between two pairs of shoes: one with long spikes for bad turf and one with short spikes for good turf. The field *appeared* to be in good condition—the grass looked green and full. So I wore the short spikes. Bad move. Because it had rained for a couple of weeks, the field was actually in poor condition. The grounds crew had painted it green, so it would look nice for the game. I only wish I had realized all this *before* it was time for me to return the opening kickoff.

I took the ball on the four-yard line, took two steps, and fell down in front of the whole stadium! I sat there with the ball gently cradled in my lap while twenty-one players stared down at me. Because I was wearing the wrong shoes, our team had to start play from scrimmage deep in our own territory. On the sidelines I even tried to find someone who didn't play as frequently to swap shoes with me, but I couldn't get any takers. As a result, I slipped all over the field.

THE BOOTS OF THE ROMAN SOLDIER

If the right kind of shoes are important in athletics, you can imagine how important they are for the soldier fighting for his life on the battlefield. During the American Revolutionary War, the soldiers under General Washington had to wrap their feet because their shoes had worn out. As a result, many soldiers became injured or lost their lives because of cold weather.

In Paul's day the footwear of choice for the Roman soldier was a thick-soled, hobnailed semiboot. It had thick leather straps that secured it to the foot. On the bottom of the sole were little pieces of metal that protruded like spikes to give the soldier firmness of footing, so he could stand in the battle. That way in hand-to-hand combat he could hold his ground and make quick moves without slipping, sliding, or falling.

The soldier's footwear was designed to provide not only sure footing but also protection for long marches covering tremendous amounts of terrain. In addition, the enemy commonly placed razor-sharp sticks in the ground in hopes of piercing the feet of the advancing soldiers. To protect themselves, soldiers would wear boots with heavy soles that couldn't be pierced. If their feet were pierced, they couldn't walk. Even the best soldier is rendered ineffective if he cannot stand up.

THE BOOTS OF THE CHRISTIAN SOLDIER

In spiritual warfare it's vital for the believer to be wearing the right kind of footwear. You can have your waist cinched up with commitment and be wearing the breastplate of holy living, but unless you have sure footing and protection, you're going to fall. That's why in Ephesians 6:15, Paul said our feet are to be shod "with the preparation of the gospel of peace."

EQUIPPED FOR BATTLE

Many assume Paul was telling us to preach the gospel. They

base that interpretation on Romans 10:15, which says, "How will they preach unless they are sent? Just as it is written, 'How beautiful are the feet of those who bring good news of good things!'"

There's no question that the gospel needs to be preached. That's what Paul was saying in Romans 10:15, but *not* in Ephesians 6:15. Here Paul is describing the armor that is our *defense*, and when he writes of "preparation of the gospel of peace," he is speaking of having *embraced* the gospel. We put on these shoes at salvation: "Having been justified by faith, we have peace with God through our Lord Jesus Christ" (Rom. 5:1). That's what enables us to stand firm.

If your feet are shod with the good news of peace, you are protected and will be able to stand your ground against the Devil (Eph. 6:13). You don't need to slip, slide, or fall when you're under attack. Since the "gospel of peace" is so effective in resisting Satan, let's make sure we understand what it refers to.

THE WAR BETWEEN GOD AND MAN

Most people, unless they're atheists, can't even conceive of themselves as being at war with God. Many claim to be religious— to believe in God and be concerned about what He thinks. They certainly don't see themselves as enemies of God actively striking blows at God's kingdom. But the Bible makes it clear that before a person comes to Christ, he or she is a sinner, an enemy of God, and an object of God's wrath and judgment (Rom. 5:8–10).

It's clear that God and humanity start out on two different sides.

The issue is not predominantly that man is at war with God, but that God is at war with man. In Romans 1:18, Paul said, "The wrath of God is revealed from heaven against all ungodliness and unrighteousness of men who suppress the truth in unrighteousness." Why is God at war? Because He is the enemy of sin and sin's father, Satan. If you are not on God's side, you are on Satan's side (Matt. 12:30; John 1:12; 8:44).

Nahum the prophet wrote:

> A jealous and avenging God is the LORD; the LORD is
> avenging and wrathful. The LORD takes vengeance on
> His adversaries, and He reserves wrath for His ene-
> mies. The LORD is slow to anger and great in power,
> and the LORD will by no means leave the guilty unpun-
> ished. (1:2–3)

Anyone who is an enemy of God will know and feel His punishment. The war is so intense that God will someday cast the
unbeliever into a lake of fire to burn for eternity (Rev. 21:8).

THE GOOD NEWS OF PEACE

Near Athens in Greece is a plain called Marathon. It is approxi-
mately five miles long and two miles wide. In 490 BC the Persian
king Darius ordered his generals to enslave the Greek cities of
Athens and Eretria. The latter was destroyed and its inhabitants
enslaved. The Persians then landed at Marathon, hoping to do the
same to Athens. The Battle of Marathon was a decisive battle, for if
the Persians had conquered, Grecian culture might never have blos-
somed in the world. Against fearful odds the Greeks were victorious.

When the enemy was defeated, Pheidippides, a Greek soldier
and courier, ran from the plains of Marathon to Athens, a distance
of slightly more than twenty-six miles, to deliver a message to the
magistrates. As he delivered his message, he fell over dead. What
was his message? That the war was over and victory had been
achieved. Today's marathon race commemorates the faithful soldier
who announced the good news of peace.

In the spiritual realm there is also good news about peace:
There is war between God and man, but God has made peace.
How? By justifying those whom He called to salvation. And "hav-
ing been justified by faith, we have peace with God through our
Lord Jesus Christ" (Rom. 5:1).

What does this peace refer to? Some suggest it is a tranquility
of the mind. But this peace is not subjective; it is objective. It does
not refer to feelings, but to a relationship. Peace with God means

we aren't on opposite sides anymore. That's the good news. The wrath of God, which ultimately could have consigned us to hell, has been removed. Our war with Him is over.

How did God reconcile us to Himself? Through the death of His Son on our behalf. Paul wrote, "God demonstrates His own love toward us, in that while we were yet sinners, Christ died for us. Much more then, having now been justified by His blood, we shall be saved from the wrath of God through Him" (Rom. 5:8–9).

God poured out His vengeance, anger, and wrath on Christ, who acted as our substitute. Christ made full payment for our sins, and God's anger was appeased. Our new status is peace with God. Because Christ bore all our sins, we are forever holy and faultless in His sight.

How does God maintain this peace? Through Christ our High Priest, who cleanses us from all sin (1 John 1:7). He maintains our relationship with Him through His past act on the cross and His present mediation at God's right hand (Heb. 7:25). In Romans 5:10, Paul said, "If while we were enemies we were reconciled to God through the death of His Son, much more, having been reconciled, we shall be saved by His life." Since a dying Savior succeeded in bringing us to God, a living Savior can certainly keep us there.

How long will God maintain this relationship of peace? Forever! In Hebrews 10:14, the writer said, "By one offering He has perfected *for all time* those who are sanctified."

SURE-FOOTEDNESS ON THE BATTLEGROUND

One evening I was called to the church, and found one of our elders contending with a demon-possessed girl. The demons used her mouth to speak, but the voices coming out of her mouth were not her own. Amazing things were going on in that room. She had flipped over a desk and was smashing other things in the room.

When I walked into the room, she suddenly sat on a chair, gave me a frenzied look, and in a voice not her own said, "Get him out! Not him! Get him out!" I was glad that the demons knew whose side I was on. At first we didn't know what to do. We tried to speak to the demons. We commanded them to tell us their names, and we ordered them in Jesus' name to go to the pit. We spent two hours trying to send those demons out of her.

When we finally stopped trying to talk to the demons and dealt directly with that young woman, we began to make some headway.

We presented the gospel to her, explaining that she needed to confess and forsake her sins. She prayed with a repentant heart, confessed her sin, and found true deliverance in salvation. By doing so, she shod her feet with "the gospel of peace." She left that night standing firm. The demons were gone and have never troubled her since.

It's wonderful to know that God is on our side. We are one with Him and fully protected in Christ. Because of that, we can stand firm in battle against Satan. There's no need to slip or slide. The sure-footed Christian has this attitude: "Satan, you can come against me, but I'll stand firm because I know God is on my side." That was the kind of sure-footedness Peter had.

THE RESOLVE OF PETER

In John 18:4–6, Peter stood with the other disciples in the garden of Gethsemane while a battalion of soldiers came at night to apprehend Christ. There were six hundred men in a battalion. They carried with them torches, lanterns, and weapons. Obviously they were expecting a struggle. When they found Christ, He asked, "Whom do you seek?"

They replied, "Jesus the Nazarene."

He said, "I am He." When Christ merely uttered those words, His enemies fell back flat on the ground.

That display of divine power impressed Peter, who drew out his sword and struck off the ear of the high priest's slave. Apparently he was thinking, *What power! Since my Lord is that powerful, there's no sense in being taken.* And I'm convinced Peter was not trying to chop off the slave's ear; he was aiming for his head. The slave must have ducked.

Peter was ready to take on the entire Roman army. Where did he get that kind of resolve? From seeing soldiers fall flat in the dirt at the name of Jesus. He sensed that nothing could defeat him because he knew the Lord was on his side.

But what Peter did was wrong. He was driven by his feelings, not by the revealed truth Christ had given him. Had Peter listened to our Lord's instructions earlier that evening, he would have known that these events were the unfolding of God's extraordinary plan.

Unfortunately, many of those today who are preoccupied with confrontational demonic warfare are on no firmer ground than Peter was that night in the garden. Their zeal is inflated with a false confidence born out of experience, not God's Word. We must test every experience with the touchstone of truth, which is God's Word. That's why the prophet Isaiah declared, "To the law and to the testimony! If they do not speak according to this word, it is because they have no dawn" (8:20).

Why did Isaiah say that? Because the Lord wanted the nation of Israel to seek Him through His Word, the only reliable source of truth, rather than consult spirits (v. 19).

Paul warned even Timothy, who was a leader and well trained in divine truth, to stay away from error and concentrate instead on the pure truth of God's Word (1 Tim. 6:20–21). To subject oneself to false teaching is to disobey God.

Dr. Peter Masters correctly addressed the issue in this way:

> When wonders and marvels wrought by the hands of
> man become a buttress to belief, then real faith is
> undermined. What a triumph for the devil if he can take
> away the faith of true Christian people so that instead
> of grounding their hope on what God has said, they
> come to depend on a constant flow of visible "proofs,"
> saying, "I must see amazing signs and wonders!" ... By
> this means the person and the Word of the eternal,
> ever-blessed God are snubbed and insulted.[1]

Don't let sensory evidence—no matter how powerfully persuasive—pull you away from the truth of God's Word.

THE OBEDIENCE OF GIDEON

Gideon learned how to stand his ground in battle against enormous odds. The army from the land of Midian invaded and attacked the nation of Israel: "The Midianites and the Amalekites and all the sons of the east were ... as numerous as locusts; and their camels were without number, as numerous as the sand on the seashore" (Judg. 7:12). In response to the Midianite oppression, Israel assembled an army of thirty-two thousand soldiers. But the Lord told Gideon he didn't need that many soldiers. Eventually, only three hundred men remained to fight the enemy (v. 6).

The Lord promised Gideon that those few men would defeat the entire army of Midian (v. 7). How? The Lord told Gideon to give each man a pitcher covering a candle, and a trumpet. Then they were to circle the army of Midian, which was encamped in the valley below them. When God gave Gideon the word, the men were to blow their trumpets, break their pitchers, and hold up their candles (vv. 16–21). When they followed the Lord's instructions, the soldiers of Midian, in all the confusion, killed one another (v. 22). Why was Gideon willing to fight an entire army with only three hundred men? He knew the Lord was on his side.

In Christ's power you also can stand with such confidence. Whatever Satan may cast against you, you have no reason to fear when your feet are shod with "the gospel of peace."

8

FAITH:
OUR DEFENSE SHIELD

༄

Anumber years ago, Fuller Theological Seminary in Pasadena, California, offered a course called MC510: The Miraculous and Church Growth. At the conclusion of each lecture, laboratory sessions were held to do such things as cast out demons and heal people. The purpose of that activity was to enable students to discover what miraculous gifts they had supposedly been given.

The course, which was both the most popular and the most disruptive course on campus, is now defunct. Several of the theological faculty raised questions about what was going on in the classroom. That protest resulted in a moratorium on the course, and the school's president then ordered a faculty task force to study the biblical, theological, and psychological impact of the course on the curriculum. The ensuing published report concluded that a course on signs and wonders was not appropriate for a theological curriculum. Here are a few of the faculty's wise objections to the course:

New secularism. [A] strong emphasis on the miraculous, stressing that God is peculiarly present in this, as distinct from natural healings, borders dangerously on an unbiblical dualism. Another version of the old "God of the gaps" dichotomy is set up in which God is at work in the extraordinary and the supernatural—but not in the ordinary and everyday.

Exclusivity. The so-called power encounter of signs and wonders was being claimed as the norm for truly biblical evangelism. The implicit, and sometimes explicit, judgment is that others have been and are doing the work of God in their own strength. Thus the great lights of the church—Augustine of Hippo, Luther, Calvin, Pascal, Jonathan Edwards, John Wesley—seem pretty dim, for the [miraculous] brand of unction was absent from their ministries.

Christian magic. Faculty were concerned that the approach to the miraculous tended to be formulaic, especially in the "deliverance" ministries, in which persons supposedly oppressed by demonic powers are set free. Some ... students stressed saying the right words or going through a list of demons' names so as to find the specific one involved in the oppression. You go down the list until one name strikes home. This approach assumes an *ipso facto* God who can be coerced to do our bidding; if we do this, then he must do that.

Privatism. When the charismatic is pushed to the front of Christian experience, the ethical tends to take a back seat. It seems those most preoccupied with physical health and demonic realities tend to be the least concerned in confronting these issues. But the ultimate goal of the Christian life is the fruit, not the gifts, of the Spirit....

Failures. What do you do with the people who are not healed? This question was foremost in the minds of many of the faculty. Did Satan win one? If so, then

Satan holds a commanding lead in the game, because
the majority of people who are prayed for do not, in
fact, get well physically. A subtle, but powerful, pressure therefore builds in the Signs and Wonders
mentality to see miracles where there are none. Some
faculty members were outraged at what they felt were
wild, unsubstantiated reports of healings coming out of
the meetings of MC510.[1]

The class may be defunct, but the movement it spawned is
stronger than ever. Known as the Third Wave,[2] this movement has
gained a worldwide following of people and churches that seek
"power encounters," including face-to-face confrontations with
demons. Third Wave teaching, together with a radical spiritual-
warfare movement that is growing among conservative evangelicals,
has raised Christians' interest in exorcism and demonic encounters
to a level unprecedented since the Middle Ages.

The whole tenor of Scripture is against such a trend. Our focus
is not to be on the powers of darkness. We're not to be preoccupied with evil, but with righteousness. The apostle Paul wrote, "I
want you to be wise in what is good and innocent in what is evil"
(Rom. 16:19).

Note that the spiritual armor Paul describes in Ephesians 6 is
not paraphernalia for an exorcist, but the simple resources for normal Christian living. We have examined three items that are to be
worn at all times: the belt, the breastplate, and the shoes. Now the
apostle mentions a different set of tools:

In addition to all, taking up the shield of faith with
which you will be able to extinguish all the flaming
arrows of the evil one. And take the helmet of salvation, and the sword of the Spirit, which is the word of
God. (Eph. 6:16–17)

Although all pieces of the armor are essential, Paul made a distinc-
tion between the first three pieces and the remaining three. The first

three are translated with the verb "to have," which indicates permanency. We are to wear those three pieces permanently as long-range preparation. The latter three are translated with the verb "to take," which indicates they are close at hand for whenever the battle ensues.

The Roman soldier would always be wearing his belt, breastplate, and shoes. But when there was a lull in the battle, he might temporarily lay aside his shield, sword, and helmet. But he would be ready to pick them up at a moment's notice.

The same principle applies in sports. For example, in baseball there is certain equipment the player uses all the time, such as his uniform, spikes, and pads. Although other things are essential for the game—such as a bat, helmet, or glove—the player doesn't use them all the time. But they are close at hand for whenever they're needed.

Similarly, in spiritual warfare there are some long-range elements of preparation and some for immediate readiness as the battle ensues. You are always to be committed to Christ, pursuing holiness and standing firm in the knowledge that God is on your side. That's plenty of protection for battle.

Yet God's spiritual arsenal provides the believer with even more weaponry. By using the remaining three pieces of armor—the shield of faith, the helmet of salvation, and the sword of the Spirit—we have double protection when the enemy's arrows come flying in mass force. For now, let's see what the shield refers to.

ROMAN SHIELDS

The Roman army used several kinds of shields, but two are prominent. One was a small round shield that curled like a giant Frisbee at the edges. A foot soldier would strap it to his left forearm. It was light, to allow the soldier great mobility on the battlefield.

In his right hand he carried his sword. In hand-to-hand combat, the soldier would strike with that sword while he parried the blows of his opponent with his shield. But that is not the kind of shield Paul was referring to in verse 16.

Instead, the Greek text reveals he was speaking of a large rectangular shield. This shield measured four and a half feet by two and a half feet. It was made out of a thick plank of wood and covered on the outside with either metal or leather. This outer covering was also very thick. The metal would deflect flaming arrows, while the leather would be treated to extinguish the fiery pitch on the arrows.

This shield played a strategic role when the Roman army was fighting a major battle. A long line of soldiers carrying these shields would stand in front of the troops. Behind them were other soldiers equipped with swords and arrows. As the army advanced toward the enemy, the soldiers in front would plant their shields side by side, creating a huge wall of protection. From behind that wall the archers would fire their arrows at the enemy. In this manner the army inched its way toward the enemy until they could engage them in hand-to-hand combat. In the spiritual realm the believer protects himself or herself from the enemy's fiery darts by using the shield of faith.

OUR SPIRITUAL SHIELD

A PRACTICAL DEFINITION OF FAITH

When missionary John Paton was translating the Scriptures for South Sea islanders, he was unable to find a word in their vocabulary for the concept of believing, trusting, or having faith. He had no idea how he would convey it. One day while he was working in his hut, a native came running into Paton's study and flopped into a chair, exhausted. He said, "It feels so good to rest my whole weight in this chair." Instantly John Paton knew he had his definition: Faith is resting your whole weight on God. That meaning helped bring a whole civilization to Christ.

The whole of Christianity is a matter of believing that God "is and that He is a rewarder of those who seek Him" (Heb. 11:6). The true Christian believes that God is the divine Author of Scripture, that Christ is God, and that Christ died, rose, and is coming again. He or she knows that by turning from sin and self and believing in Christ he or she will enter into His kingdom. In Habakkuk 2:4, the Lord stated it simply: "The righteous will live by his faith."

Faith is trusting completely and unconditionally in God and His Word. True faith doesn't need to ask any questions or seek any explanations. Why did men such as Abel, Enoch, Noah, Abraham, and Moses believe in God? Because they had a right view of who He is. They focused on God and His character. They had such an exalted view of the sovereign God that they took Him at His Word.

The author of Hebrews characterized faith in this way: "Faith is the assurance of things hoped for, the conviction of things not seen" (11:1). The Greek word here translated "assurance" appears two other times in the book of Hebrews. In 1:3, it speaks of Christ's being the very essence of the Father. In 3:14, it refers to a guarantee. Faith is the assurance that God's promises have essence, content, and reality.

Referring to the time of Abraham, the author of Hebrews said, "All these died in faith, without receiving the promises, but having seen them and having welcomed them from a distance, and having confessed that they were strangers and exiles on the earth" (11:13). Although the Old Testament patriarchs died before all God's promises to them were fulfilled, their lives were characterized by a continual trust that God would keep His promises. They saw heaven with the eye of faith, regarding themselves as pilgrims going to a city "whose architect and builder is God" (v. 10).

Faith also provides conviction about unseen realities (v. 1). Faith is living on the basis of things not seen. In response to the reaction Thomas had when he first saw Jesus after He was raised from the dead, Christ said, "Because you have seen Me, have you believed? Blessed are they who did not see, and yet believed" (John 20:29). As Christians we worship "Him who is unseen" (Heb. 11:27).

FAITH'S COMPANION

As believers we are to exercise our faith. That is the definition of obedience.

Joshua, the leader of Israel, is a good illustration of obedient faith. He was given what seemed like an impossible mission: conquering the mighty city of Jericho.

The Canaanites used Jericho as a frontier fortress to defend their land. The city was surrounded by massive walls so wide that two chariots could run side by side along the top. The Israelites had good reason for fearing the Canaanites. They were fierce warriors and mighty men. Years earlier Moses had sent spies into Canaan on a reconnaissance mission. When they came back, the majority of them advised against going into the land because they claimed its inhabitants were too big (Num. 13:33).

Taking the city of Jericho was an unprecedented exercise of faith. Israel had no army and no weapons. For forty years they had wandered in the desert. Now they were to go against a city that was walled, barred, and fortified. But Jericho was the gateway to the Promised Land, and they had to conquer it.

God told Joshua to have the Israelites walk around the city once and then return to their camp. They were to do that for six days in a row. On the seventh day they were to walk around the city seven times and blow their horns and shout with all their might.

It took faith to follow through with God's plan. Why? First, it was embarrassing. All they did at first was walk around. Second, it was dangerous: The Canaanites could shoot arrows at them or drop rocks or hot liquid from the wall. From a human perspective the plan appeared ridiculous. But the people obeyed God. On the seventh day they marched around the city seven times, and then they shouted. Hebrews 11:30 describes the result in this way: "By faith the walls of Jericho fell down after they had been encircled for seven days." It was faith, not folly, because they were obeying God.

One pastor erroneously cited that great triumph as an example of how we are to conquer territorial demons:

> Spying out the land is essential when warring for a city.... Christians should walk or drive every major freeway, avenue and road of their cities, praying and coming against demonic strongholds over every neighborhood....
>
> Even if you don't see instant results, keep the trumpets blowing.... Always remember, God is not slack concerning His promise; the walls will come down![3]

That is folly, not faith, because God has given no such command. Driving every major freeway, avenue, and road would be a major undertaking, especially in a large city. In a city like Los Angeles it would probably take full-time drivers several years to cover all the roads. That method seems especially slow since it can take hours or weeks for a pastor just in his office to "deliver" a person from demons. And to issue commands successfully as you are driving would necessitate unusually cooperative freeway demons! After all, why should they decide to listen to you—especially if you're whizzing by at fifty-five miles per hour?

The Israelites conquered Jericho because God told them to. Nowhere in His Word does He instruct believers to spy out neighborhoods and do a drive-by to zap demons. Our instructions are clear; Christ simply said, "Go into all the world and *preach the gospel* to all creation" (Mark 16:15).

Our Lord explained further that you need to "let your light shine before men in such a way that they may see your good works, and glorify your Father who is in heaven" (Matt. 5:16). "Good" refers to an attractiveness or a beautiful appearance. Letting your light shine before others allows them to see the beauty the Lord has worked in you.

Are we to keep the trumpets blowing? Will the walls always come down, as that pastor claimed? The walls in Jericho fell down immediately because God said they would. But it is not always God's purpose to have walls fall down. Often He allows barriers or obstacles to remain as a way of testing the believer's faith. Note that never again did the Israelites conquer a city by the method they used at Jericho.

TORTURED FAITH

When faith is exhibited in the face of trials, its authenticity is proved. Martyn Lloyd-Jones was right when he said:

> Faith is many-sided. There is generally at the beginning
> a good deal of admixture in what we call our faith; there

is a good deal of the flesh that we are not aware of. And
as we begin to learn these things, and as we go on with
the process, God puts us through His testing times. He
tests us by trials as if by fire in order that the things
which do not belong to the essence of faith may fall off.

We may think that our faith is perfect and that we
can stand up against anything. Then suddenly a trial
comes and we find that we fail. Why? Well that is just
an indication that the trust element in our faith needs
to be developed.... The more we experience these
things [trials], the more we learn to trust God.[4]

Faith that conquers is great faith, but faith that continues is
even greater. It's true that many Old Testament heroes "by faith
conquered kingdoms, performed acts of righteousness, obtained
promises, shut the mouths of lions, quenched the power of fire,
escaped the edge of the sword, from weakness were made strong,
became mighty in war, put foreign armies to flight" (Heb.
11:33–34). But that was not true for everyone, for the passage
continues:

Others were tortured, not accepting their release, so
that they might obtain a better resurrection; and others
experienced mockings and scourgings, yes, also chains
and imprisonment. They were stoned, they were sawn
in two, they were tempted, they were put to death
with the sword; they went about in sheepskins, in
goatskins, being destitute, afflicted, ill-treated (men of
whom the world was not worthy), wandering in
deserts and mountains and caves and holes in the
ground. (vv. 35–38)

If they had recanted their faith, they would have been delivered.
But they endured suffering because they were looking for a heavenly and eternal deliverance, not an earthly and temporal one. They
did not fear death, for they knew the final resurrection would

clothe their bodies in immortality. They viewed their trials through the eye of faith. May the Lord help us see our trials the same way.

THE ENEMY'S INCOMING ARROWS

In Paul's day archers of the Roman army would put a cottonlike material on the tip of their arrows and soak it in pitch. Before they shot the arrow, they would light it. It would burn slowly but was very hot. When the arrow hit its target, the pitch would splatter and start little fires on the clothing of the soldier or on a wooden target.

In spiritual warfare we are to take the shield of faith "to extinguish all the flaming arrows of the evil one" (Eph. 6:16). What are Satan's "flaming arrows"?

TEMPTATION IN THE DESERT

Satan launched flaming arrows against Christ as He was preparing for ministry (Matt. 4:1). Christ had fasted for forty days and nights (v. 2). At the end of that time, Satan tempted Him to disbelieve God.

In the first temptation Satan challenged Christ to turn stones into bread (v. 3). The Devil was saying, "God claimed He would take care of and sustain You. But You've been in the wilderness with nothing to eat for forty days. Looks like God has abandoned You. Since You're the Son of God, why not grab some satisfaction? Don't wait around for God anymore. He's surely forgotten You by now." Satan was tempting Him to distrust God and take control of His destiny.

In the next temptation Satan took Christ to the pinnacle of the temple in Jerusalem and said to Him, "If You are the Son of God, throw Yourself down" (v. 6). Satan was saying, "Didn't God promise to make You the Messiah? Didn't He promise that every knee would bow before You? Didn't He promise that You would be King and receive homage and worship? Come with me. We'll go to the top of the temple, and You can dive off it. Angels will protect You, and the people will know You are the Messiah" (see vv. 5–6).

In the third temptation Satan took Christ to a high mountain and showed Him all the kingdoms of the world. Then Satan said, "All these things will I give You, if You fall down and worship me" (v. 9). What was Satan saying? "Didn't God tell You He would give You the kingdoms of the world? Come with me, and I will give them to You now" (see vv. 8–9). Satan was implying that you can't count on God to keep His Word.

TEMPTATION IN THE GARDEN

Satan will try to deceive us in the same way. That's evident from what took place in the garden of Eden. God created a perfect environment. He also created a perfect man and woman—perfect in the sense of sinlessness, but not in the sense of proven perfection. So Satan, disguised as a serpent, said to Eve, "Did God really say …?" (Gen. 3:1 NIV). Satan wanted her to doubt God.

Then Satan lied to Eve, saying, "You surely will not die! For God knows that in the day you eat from [the Tree of the Knowledge of Good and Evil] your eyes will be opened, and you will be like God, knowing good and evil" (vv. 4–5). Satan was saying, "You can't trust God because He has ulterior motives. It's just that He doesn't like competition." What happened? Eve believed Satan. Ever since, the Devil has tempted people to believe him instead of God.

Satan will fire shafts of impurity, selfishness, doubt, fear, disappointment, lust, greed, vanity, and covetousness. Those temptations are all part of the lust of the flesh, the lust of the eyes, and the pride of life (1 John 2:16). Satan literally bombards his opponents with the fiery darts of seductive temptation to illicit, ungodly responses.

Satan will say, "I know the Bible says you're not supposed to have sexual relationships outside of marriage, but trust me: It's fun." Many fall to that temptation. One man who professed to be a Christian claimed he had over fifty sexual involvements and wasn't married. He said, "Christ wants us to live abundant lives; to me that includes sex."[5] Who is he believing? Not God.

So many have said to me, "I know the Bible says I should marry only a Christian. But I have a wonderful relationship with someone who isn't a Christian. We're getting married, and I'm trusting that the Lord will do a saving work. After all, the Lord is gracious." That isn't faith; it's disobedience. God says don't do it; Satan says do it. God says, "Don't read that lewd magazine; don't watch that obscene film; don't cheat on your income tax; don't claim something you don't have on your expense account." Satan says, "Do it. You'll get more money, and you'll have more thrills." Satan wants us to believe his way brings fulfillment and satisfaction, but he is a liar (John 8:44).

In the heat of battle how are we to defend ourselves against Satan? By using the shield of faith.

EMPLOYING OUR DEFENSE SHIELD

The only way to quench Satan's flaming arrows is to believe God. In Proverbs 30:5–6, the writer said, "Every word of God is tested; He is a shield to those who take refuge in Him. Do not add to His words or He will reprove you, and you will be proved a liar." What God says is true. Satan says, "I know God said that, but let me add this." No. God is a shield to those who put their trust in Him.

As long as you believe God, your shield is up. When Satan lies and you believe it, then the shield comes down. Trust God in everything. The apostle John wrote, "Whatever is born of God overcomes the world; and this is the victory that has overcome the world—our faith" (1 John 5:4). We win by trusting in God. Even though Satan hurls his flaming arrows at you, you will find strength by believing in His Word.

In 1 Corinthians 10:13, Paul said, "No temptation has overtaken you but such as is common to man; and God is faithful, who will not allow you to be tempted beyond what you are able, but with the temptation will provide the way of escape also, so that you will be able to endure it."

What will happen when you employ your defense shield? Obedience and blessing. For example, the psalmist wrote:

> How blessed are those whose way is blameless, who
> walk in the law of the LORD. How blessed are those

who observe His testimonies, who seek Him with all
their heart. They also do no unrighteousness; they
walk in His ways. You have ordained Your precepts,
that we should keep them diligently. (Ps. 119:1–4)

God wants to open the windows of heaven and pour out spiritual blessings on you. He wants to bless you abundantly. But you
must believe and obey Him, so He can do so.

What is God's battle plan? Not a so-called power encounter.
Not zapping the demons on the road. It is simply this: consistently
trusting and applying what you know to be true about God to the
issues of life.

If you don't trust God, you don't know Him well enough. The
more you know God—through studying His Word, meditating on
His majestic person, and praying to Him—the more you will trust
Him. If you love Him with all your heart, soul, mind, and strength,
and believe He is who He claims to be, and that all His promises
are true, you will stand in the place of greatest blessing.

When the flaming arrows come, grab your shield by trusting
God implicitly. There's no reason to lose the battle, for "we overwhelmingly conquer through Him who loved us" (Rom. 8:37).

THE BELIEVER'S
FUTURE GLORY

Ↄ·ↄ

I received this letter from a man who listens to our radio program in Boston:

> I am a young man of twenty-three years and came to Jesus Christ at the age of nineteen. In that time I have grown in the Word, staggered, fallen down, been crushed, been convinced by a neurotic legalist that I was demon-possessed, been arrested for driving under the influence of alcohol, and gotten a woman friend pregnant.
>
> I have begun to regain my spiritual senses. Please send me some ammunition and prayer support. The battle lines are drawn, the trenches are being dug, and I am not going to be one of those caught shame-faced when our Commanding Officer returns. When the record is being reviewed, I want it written that the soldier in

question, after repeatedly disobeying orders and going
AWOL during wartime alert, donned his armor,
reported back to his Commanding Officer, fought
courageously and fearlessly without batting an eye, and
hit the enemy with everything he could get his hands on
and inflicted heavy damage in strategic areas to the
credit of his patient, forgiving Commanding Officer.

He's been in the battle! So have you and I. As believers we will
be withstood, sidetracked, attacked, and thwarted by Satan on
every side. What are we to do? In Ephesians 6:17, Paul said, "Take
the helmet of salvation." That's the only way to persevere when the
battle gets hot.

In Roman times helmets were made out of two things: solid-
cast metal or leather with patches of metal. The helmet protected
the soldier's head from arrows, but its primary function was to
ward off blows from a broadsword. This sword was three to four
feet long and had a massive handle that was held with both hands
like a baseball bat. The soldier was to lift it over his head and bring
it down on his opponent's head. A helmet was necessary to deflect
such a crushing blow to the skull.

In the spiritual realm it's just as necessary for the believer to wear
the helmet of salvation. What does "salvation" refer to? There are
three possibilities: the past, present, or future aspects of salvation.

The past aspect of salvation is freedom from the *penalties* of sin.
If you were to ask me, "Are you a Christian?" I would reply, "Yes.
Years ago I confessed Christ as my Lord and Savior and surrendered
my life to Him. At that moment my sins were placed on the cross,
and my penalty for those sins was paid—I died to sin." Paul said it
in this way: "I have been crucified with Christ; and it is no longer
I who live, but Christ lives in me" (Gal. 2:20). When you put your
faith in Christ, you were in a spiritual sense crucified with Him, and
the penalty for sin was paid.

The present aspect of salvation means freedom from the over-
whelming *power* of sin. Sin no longer has dominion over the
believer. In Romans 6:11–14, Paul wrote:

> Consider yourselves to be dead to sin, but alive to God
> in Christ Jesus. Therefore do not let sin reign in your
> mortal body so that you obey its lusts, and do not go
> on presenting the members of your body to sin as
> instruments of unrighteousness; but present yourselves
> to God as those alive from the dead, and your members
> as instruments of righteousness to God. For sin shall
> not be master over you, for you are not under law but
> under grace.

Paul was picturing sin as a king who rules over the life of the unbeliever. But for the believer, sin is a dethroned monarch because Christ's death forever broke its power. Satan, however, doesn't want us to believe that sin's rule has been broken. He would rather have us believe he and his forces are in control. He wants sin to have the upper hand by having us think it is irresistible.

But sin has no right to rule in the believer's life. Although it desires to lure us back into its grasp, we can choose not to sin (v. 12). We are never forced to sin, nor are we unfortunate victims of inherent weaknesses that cannot be conquered. Although we will continue to struggle with sin in this fallen world, it no longer rules over us. The controlling force in our lives now is grace and holiness.

The future aspect of salvation speaks of freedom from the *presence* of sin. A day is coming when there will be no more sin. The apostle Paul wrote, "I consider that the sufferings of this present time are not worthy to be compared with the glory that is to be revealed to us" (Rom. 8:18). Someday our bodies will be saved along with our souls. That is the culmination of our salvation.

Salvation has happened—that's justification; it is happening now—that's sanctification; and it will happen in the future—that's glorification. Since salvation is past, it has been accomplished. Since it is present, it is an ongoing reality. And since it is guaranteed in the future, you are absolutely secure.

Which aspect does the helmet refer to? Not the past aspect. Paul was not saying, "After girding your loins with truth, donning the breastplate of righteousness, shodding your feet with the gospel of peace, and taking up the shield of faith, you should—by the way—go get saved." No, the past aspect of salvation is already a reality. You're not in the army unless you're a believer. If you're fighting Satan, you have to be on God's side. If you're not for Him, you're against Him (Matt. 12:30).

So what does the helmet refer to? The present and future aspects of our salvation. It is both the assurance of God's continuing work in your life and confidence in a full, final salvation to come. Note that Paul also referred to the helmet of salvation in 1 Thessalonians 5:8–9:

> Since we are of the day, let us be sober, having put on
> the breastplate of faith and love, and as a helmet, the
> hope of salvation. For God has not destined us for
> wrath, but for obtaining salvation through our Lord
> Jesus Christ.

The night is Satan's dominion. We are of the day; we are sons of light in God's kingdom. We walk in the light even now, and the future consummation of our salvation is the antithesis of God's wrath on the impenitent. God is moving us to ultimate salvation, not destruction.

THE MOTIVATION TO PERSEVERE

Knowing there is an end to spiritual warfare provides motivation for persevering in battle. We will not have to fight the world, the flesh, and the Devil forever. If salvation were only a past-tense reality, how could we ever rest in hope?

Living without hope would be like running a race without a finish line. It would be ridiculous for someone to say, "Start running for the rest of your life. There's no finish, but give it everything you've got." What kind of incentive do you have to follow through with such a request? Can you imagine God making such a pointless request? In Revelation 14:13, John said when the saints die, they rest from their labors.

If there were no guarantee of future salvation, the past aspect would be meaningless. That's the point Paul was making when he said, "If from human motives I fought with wild beasts at Ephesus, what does it profit me? If the dead are not raised, let us eat and drink, for tomorrow we die" (1 Cor. 15:32). He was saying, "Do you think I'm going to lay my life on the line by confronting hostile pagans with Christ's gospel if there's no resurrection? I would give up right now and throw in the towel!" A salvation with no future leaves the soldier powerless to fight the battle today.

But Paul didn't throw in the towel. He was "afflicted in every way, but not crushed; perplexed, but not despairing; persecuted, but not forsaken; struck down, but not destroyed" (2 Cor. 4:8–9). Paul lived day to day on the edge of death while confronting a godless, hostile world. Why? Because he knew that someday for sure he would be raised to glory with Christ (v. 14). He had his helmet firmly in place.

A REASON TO REJOICE

The helmet enables us to *endure* trials, not *escape* them. Too many people today are seeking to avoid trials rather than persevere in them. Unfortunately, some of the most popular teaching in the spiritual-warfare movement caters to this misguided longing. The reasoning goes like this: "Since Satan causes disease, and Christ came to destroy Satan's work, it must therefore be God's will to heal disease." Their implication is that God does not use sickness for the spiritual benefit of believers. One professor wrote:

> Disease is never seen as something that God sends for our character development or growth. Disease is never said to develop such Christian virtues as patience, long-suffering, trust or faith, but rather something that in extreme cases God may use to stop our descent into further sin....
>
> Sickness in the New Testament is viewed negatively. It is not sent by God, except for punishment of sin, and that is a rare occurrence....
>
> Sickness is to be healed. It is never welcomed, but always prayed against.... There is no hint that continuing in sickness is in itself beneficial.[1]

Is it true that God never sends sickness and disease to develop our spiritual growth? Is punishment for sin the only reason God sends sickness? Is sickness never to be welcomed? Is a believer who is sick or diseased outside God's perfect will? Perish the thought!

In his article "Poor Health May Be the Best Remedy" J. I. Packer correctly addressed the issue in this way:

> Perfect physical health is promised, not for this life, but for heaven, as part of the resurrection glory that awaits us in the day when Christ "will change our lowly body to be like his glorious body, by the power which enables him even to subject all things to himself." Full bodily well-being is set forth as a future blessing of salvation rather than a present one. What God has promised, and when he will give it, are separate questions.[2]

Paul spoke of that future blessing of salvation in this way: "We exult in hope of the glory of God" (Rom. 5:2). This verse speaks of a confident boast or exultant jubilation, of rejoicing at the highest level. What is it we're to rejoice in so greatly? The hope of glorification. That hope is not based on our own worthiness, but on the promise and power of God (8:11). We look forward to one day losing our humanness—our earthiness—and becoming glorified persons. The consummation of our redemption and the ultimate fulfillment of our salvation are the manifestation of God's glory in us. We can rejoice because someday God will, in the fullest and purest way, reflect His eternal character through us.

But Paul did not end there, for he wrote, "We also exult in our tribulations, knowing that tribulation brings about perseverance; and perseverance, proven character; and proven character, hope" (5:3–4).

The believer who rejoices in future glory can also rejoice in present affliction. Why? Because trials produce the kind of character that has a greater capacity to rejoice about the future. The Greek word for "tribulations" means "pressure." It pictures squeezing olives for oil or grapes for wine. No matter how severe or devastating our trials are, they can never take away our hope of future glory or steal our joy. It's no wonder the writer of Hebrews called such hope an anchor of the soul (6:19).

In her book *A Step Further* Joni Eareckson Tada wrote:

> No, Satan doesn't sneak out and cause pneumonia and cancer while God happens to be looking the other way listening to the prayers of His saints. He can only do what our all-powerful and all-knowing God allows him to do. And we have God's promise that nothing will be allowed which is not for our good or which is too hard for us to bear (Rom. 8:28; 1 Cor. 10:13)....
>
> Praise God that when Satan causes us illness—or any calamity—we can answer him with the words Joseph answered his brothers who sold him into slavery, "As for you, you meant evil against me, but God meant it for good" (Gen. 50:20).
>
> I sometimes shudder to think where I would be today if I had not broken my neck. I couldn't see at first why God would possibly allow it, but I sure do now. He has gotten so much more glory through my paralysis than through my health! And believe me, you'll never know how rich that makes me feel. If God chooses to heal you in answer to prayer, that's great. Thank Him for it. But if He chooses not to, thank Him anyway. You can be sure He has His reasons.[3]

Why can we be thankful for sickness, disease, and other trials? Because Romans 5:3–4 tells us they are spiritually beneficial. First, they produce perseverance. By experiencing trials you learn to trust God and His sustaining power (2 Cor. 12:7–10). Second, they prove your spiritual character by purifying and strengthening you. Going through a trial is like spiritual weight lifting—it builds your spiritual muscles and produces a greater level of holiness.

Finally, trials produce hope, "and hope does not disappoint, because the love of God has been poured out within our hearts through the Holy Spirit who was given to us" (Rom. 5:5). Professor John Murray wrote:

> "The love of God" is not our love to God but God's love to us.... What is it that gives solidity to this hope and guarantees its validity? It is the love of God to believers, a love that suffers no fluctuation or reverse. Hence the hope which it promises is as irreversible as the love itself.[4]

Are you undergoing trials on the battlefield of life? Be encouraged, for "the sufferings of this present time are not worthy to be compared with the glory that is to be revealed to us" (Rom. 8:18).

THE FIGHT AGAINST DISCOURAGEMENT

The Roman soldier wore his helmet to defend himself against a broadsword. In spiritual warfare Satan's broadsword has two sides to it: discouragement and doubt.

His attacks of discouragement might go like this: "You sure are giving a lot and not getting much in return. You're conforming your life to the standard of God's Word and setting yourself apart from the world. But what happens? You just lost your job! Some blessing! You've been reading your Bible every day, but your wife is as cranky as she was before you bought it, and it hasn't had any effect on her. What is God doing in your life? You've been going to church for years, but look at your children. They don't respect you today any more than they ever did."

Some are discouraged because they become weary. You might be thinking, *Do I have to disciple another person? Can't I have a few days off from reading my Bible? I can't handle that Sunday school class another Sunday! Lord, I don't have to talk to my neighbor another time, do I? Lord, You know I've been fighting this same temptation a long time; I'm getting tired.*

Perhaps you are discouraged because of an unbelieving spouse who seemingly will never change. Maybe you don't receive the thanks you ought to for your ministry. Perhaps you have a physical infirmity that causes you to grow tired of struggling. Those things are precisely what the helmet is for. Don't look at present circumstances. Cling to the hope of eternal salvation and the glory that will be yours.

In the book of 1 Kings the writer described how Elijah, a prophet of God, became discouraged. He had just experienced a great victory by killing 450 priests of Baal (18:22, 40). But then there was a quick turn of events:

> Ahab [the king of Israel] told Jezebel [his wife] all that
> Elijah had done, and how he had killed all the prophets
> with the sword. Then Jezebel sent a messenger to
> Elijah, saying, "So may the gods do to me and even
> more, if I do not make your life as the life of one of
> them by tomorrow about this time." (19:1–2)

Jezebel was a Baal worshipper. Because of what Elijah did to her priests, she was determined to kill him by the next day or die trying. Now if Elijah could handle 450 priests of Baal, you would think one woman wouldn't shake him. But he decided the only thing to do was run:

> He [Elijah] was afraid and arose and ran for his life and
> came to Beersheba, which belongs to Judah, and left his
> servant there. But he himself went a day's journey into
> the wilderness, and came and sat down under a juniper
> tree; and he requested for himself that he might die,
> and said, "It is enough; now, O LORD, take my life, for
> I am not better than my fathers." (vv. 3–4)

Elijah might have been thinking, *Lord, I just did You a big favor by eliminating the priests of Baal. Then You send Jezebel after me the next day. How about a little rest?* He actually wanted to die. Now that's what I call discouragement!

When Satan tries to debilitate you with his sword of discouragement, remember this: "Salvation is nearer to us than when we believed" (Rom. 13:11). Don't give up! The end of the war is near. Your service for Christ is not in vain (1 Cor. 15:58).

A true test of character is what it takes to stop a person. Many people hit the first line of defense and bail out. But there are those who make a difference in this world because they go right through line after line after line of opposition.

What about you? Have you ever felt as though you couldn't go on? Have you ever reached the place where you were about to faint? Have you ever said, "Lord, I don't have any strength left"?

You can fight all the way by putting on the helmet of salvation. Remember these basic truths:

> *We will be like Christ:* "We know that when He appears, we
>   will be like Him, because we will see Him just as
>   He is" (1 John 3:2).
> *We will enjoy endless companionship with Christ:* Jesus said,
>   "I will come again and receive you to Myself, that
>   where I am, there you may be also" (John 14:3).
> *We will enjoy complete health:* Our perishable body "is
>   raised an imperishable body; it is sown in dis-
>   honor, it is raised in glory; it is sown in weakness,
>   it is raised in power" (1 Cor. 15:42–43).
> *We will enjoy unending happiness:* God "will wipe away
>   every tear from their eyes; and there will no longer
>   be any death; there will no longer be any mourn-
>   ing, or crying, or pain" (Rev. 21:4).

A great day of victory is coming. Therefore don't let Satan discourage you. Don't let him take away the hope that helps you persevere. Someday the glorious light of Christ's presence will burst upon you. If you keep fighting now, you'll be able to report then, "Lord, I may be bruised and bleeding, but I'm here. I fought all the way."

THE FIGHT AGAINST DOUBT

Besides discouragement, Satan has another edge on his sword:

doubt. Do you know that he wants you to doubt your salvation? He is good at that. Most people suffer a lack of assurance at some point in their Christian life. After you have sinned, Satan will say, "You're not a Christian. Why would the Lord ever save you? You'll never make it—you're not good enough. You don't deserve to be saved."

Some people say you can lose your salvation. Others believe no one can really be certain he is saved until he meets the Lord. Unbiblical teaching like that causes people to live in a constant state of insecurity. What a horrible existence! That would be opposite of 1 John 1:4: "These things write we ... that your joy may be full" (KJV). Or 5:13: "These things I have written to you who believe ... so that you may *know* that you have eternal life."

Some people believe a Christian loses his salvation every time he sins. On a supposedly Christian call-in program, I heard a caller ask, "If you sin as a Christian, but forget to confess it before Christ comes, what happens?" The host responded, "You'll go to hell." Can you imagine living under that kind of fear?

Why does Satan want us to doubt our salvation? Because he wants us to doubt God's promises. He wants us to believe that God doesn't keep His Word. He wants us to believe that God won't hold on to us forever. He wants us to deny God's power and think that God's a liar. He knows that, in effect, if we doubt our salvation, we have removed our helmet.

Please don't misunderstand—there *is* a place for legitimate self-examination. Paul wrote, "Test yourselves to see if you are in the faith; examine yourselves! Or do you not recognize this about yourselves, that Jesus Christ is in you—unless indeed you fail the test?" (2 Cor. 13:5). Peter likewise wrote, "Therefore, brethren, be all the more diligent to make certain about His calling and choosing you" (2 Peter 1:10). We're commanded to examine ourselves every time we partake of the Lord's Table (1 Cor. 11:28). But the purpose of that self-examination is not to revel in doubt, but to "know ... that we are of the truth, and ... assure our heart before Him" (1 John 3:19)—another way of saying "put on the helmet."

As we have seen, our salvation has past, present, and future implications. Paul wrote, "I am confident of this very thing, that He who began a good work in you [past aspect of salvation] will perfect

it [present aspect] until the day of Christ Jesus [future aspect]"
(Phil. 1:6). Christ Himself said in John 6: "All that the Father gives
Me will come to Me, and the one who comes to Me I will certainly
not cast out" (v. 37). Surely those promises are enough to ward off
the Enemy's blows of discouragement and doubt!

We who know Christ are gifts from the Father to the Son—
tokens of the Father's love. The Son securely holds those the Father
gives to Him. Under no circumstances will Christ give them up or
turn them away, for He said,

> I have come down from heaven, not to do My own will,
> but the will of Him who sent Me. This is the will of
> Him who sent Me, that of all that He has given Me I
> lose nothing, but raise it up on the last day. (vv. 38–39)

God's calling cannot be revoked, His inheritance cannot be
defiled, His foundation cannot be shaken, and His seal cannot
be broken. Because that is so, there's no need for believers to
fear Satan's assaults. Our future glorification is divinely assured.

In John 10:27–29 Christ gives this picture of the believer's
eternal security:

> My sheep hear My voice, and I know them, and they
> follow Me; and I give eternal life to them, and they will
> never perish; and no one will snatch them out of My
> hand. My Father, who has given them to Me, is greater
> than all; and no one is able to snatch them out of the
> Father's hand.

Those verses describe seven strands in a heavenly rope that
binds us eternally to Christ. What are they?

The first is the character of the Shepherd. Since we belong to
Him, it's His duty as a Shepherd to protect and care for us. If He
were to lose us, He would violate His divine character and ability.

Another strand is the character of the sheep. In verse 27, He
said His sheep follow Him without exception. They will not listen

to strangers; they will listen only to Him. Although they occasionally stumble and sin, they know whom to follow.

Another strand is the definition of eternal life. In verse 28, Christ said, "I give eternal life to them." How long does eternal life last? Forever. To speak of it as ending is a contradiction in terms. We are secure by the very definition of eternal life.

Still another strand is that eternal life is a gift. We didn't do anything to earn eternal life, and we can't do anything to keep it. It is a gift.

Verse 28 continues, "They will never perish." That's the strand of Christ's truthfulness. If believers were to perish, that would make Christ a liar. But God cannot lie (Titus 1:2). What He says is trustworthy.

Another strand is the power of Christ. Christ said, "No one will snatch them out of My hand" (John 10:28). Leon Morris well pointed out:

> It is one of the precious things about the Christian faith
> that our continuance in eternal life depends not on our
> feeble hold on Christ, but on His firm grip on us.[5]

The final strand is the power of the Father. Christ said, "My Father, who has given them to Me, is greater than all; and no one is able to snatch them out of the Father's hand" (v. 29). Notice that in verse 28 Christ said, "My hand," and in verse 29 "the Father's hand." Now that's double protection!

What was Christ saying? That nothing or no one can rescind God's salvation or snatch you from His shepherding hand. Paul expressed the same thing:

> I am convinced that neither death, nor life, nor angels,
> nor principalities, nor things present, nor things to
> come, nor powers, nor height, nor depth, nor any
> other created thing, will be able to separate us from
> the love of God, which is in Christ Jesus our Lord.
> (Rom. 8:38–39)

If you are a genuine believer, don't allow Satan to plague you with doubts. Your salvation, which includes future glory, is eternally secure in Christ. Wear that as your helmet!

PERSEVERING IN THE MIDST OF EVIL

Sometimes the battle really gets hot and heavy. That's what motivated Jude to write his letter, which is about apostasy or a departure from the faith. An apostate is not a believer who turns from faith, but a false professor whose lack of faith causes him to turn away. Jude characterized apostate false teachers as dreamers (v. 8); prophets of greed (v. 11); clouds without water; autumn trees without fruit, doubly dead, uprooted (v. 12); wild waves of the sea; and wandering stars, for whom the black darkness has been reserved forever (v. 13). In verse 16, Jude said apostates grumble, find fault, follow after their own lusts, speak arrogantly, and flatter people for the sake of gaining an advantage.

GOD'S PROTECTION

In the midst of that apostasy and wickedness there was a group of true believers. Not only did they see false teaching and corruption coming into the church, but also all the values of society going down the drain. Undoubtedly they were apprehensive about being swept away by all that wickedness. But Jude wrote that there was no reason to fear because true believers are "the called, beloved in God the Father, and kept for Jesus Christ" (v. 1).

The Greek term used stresses a watchful care to guard something as cherished as a priceless treasure. What was Jude saying? That Christ guards us from all evil.

Apparently those in today's spiritual-warfare movement do not believe that is so. They claim, for example, that demons can inhabit a true Christian because of *ancestral involvement, personal involvement,* or *transferral.* One professor explained those terms in this way:

By *ancestral involvement* we refer to occult or demonic practices of the client's ancestors. This has been found to be one of the most common reasons for demonic affliction or demonization.[6]

He based that statement on God's instruction to the nation of Israel in Exodus 20:4–5:

> You shall not make for yourself an idol, or any likeness of what is in heaven above or on the earth beneath or in the water under the earth. You shall not worship them or serve them; for I, the LORD your God, am a jealous God, *visiting the iniquity of the fathers on the children, on the third and the fourth generations* of those who hate Me.

He continued:

> Both the idolaters and their descendants to the third and fourth generations are judged for this heinous crime, and this judgment may include actual demonization. This, too, has been borne out in history and in clinical investigation.[7]

He then defined the second and third terms in this way:

> By *personal involvement* we mean that the troubled person has himself experimented or been seriously involved in occult or demonic practices. This giving of oneself over to such forbidden practices invites the influence or invasion by demons....
>
> By *transferral* we mean that an afflicted person has come under the domination of demons by the influence of someone already demonized. To submit to that person's authority in certain situations is to submit to demonic authority.[8]

What about his statements? Can a believer inherit demons from
his ancestors? Does past involvement in the occult leave a believer
open to demonic invasion? Can demons be transferred to a believer?
Absolutely not!

As we noted previously, demons may *externally* afflict a true
believer—only by God's permission to accomplish His sovereign
purposes, however—but they can never inhabit a true believer:

> The Christian cannot be demon-possessed. Such a
> notion contradicts everything which the New Testament
> has to say concerning the nature of the new birth and
> the standing of the child of God. "It is impossible," says
> Martin Luther, "for Jesus and the devil ever to remain
> under the same roof. The one must yield to the other—
> the devil to Christ."[9]

Furthermore, Exodus 20:5 does *not* teach that the third and
fourth generations inherit the sins of their ancestors. Quite the contrary, the Old Testament is emphatic about the principle of individual
responsibility:

> Fathers shall not be put to death for their sons, nor
> shall sons be put to death for their fathers; everyone
> shall be put to death for his own sin. (Deut. 24:16)

> Yet you say, "Why should the son not bear the punishment
> for the father's iniquity?" When the son has practiced jus-
> tice and righteousness and has observed all My statutes
> and done them, he shall surely live. The person who sins
> will die. The son will not bear the punishment for the
> father's iniquity, nor will the father bear the punishment
> for the son's iniquity; the righteousness of the righteous
> will be upon himself, and the wickedness of the wicked will
> be upon himself. (Ezek. 18:19–20)

When God visits iniquity on three and four generations in a row, it is because each successive generation *chooses* to sin against God, not because its ancestors had done so.

Nowhere in the Bible is there an example of a true believer who inherited demons from his ancestors. Nowhere in the Bible is there an example of a true believer who was ever invaded by demons because of former occult practices. Nowhere in the Bible is there an example of a true believer who was inhabited by demons because of a transfer. Nowhere does the New Testament instruct the church to deliver a believer in Christ from demons because of ancestral involvement, personal involvement, transferral, or any other reason. And nowhere does the Bible say a true believer ever needs or is to seek such a deliverance. Why? Because God provides both deliverance and divine protection in salvation.

The apostle Paul expressed it in this way: "The Lord is faithful, and He will strengthen and protect you from the evil one" (2 Thess. 3:3). In 2 Timothy 1:12 he echoed the same truth: "I know whom I have believed and I am convinced that He is able to guard what I have entrusted to Him until that day." Paul was sustained by his intimate relationship with God. He personally knew the One in whom he placed his trust. What did he entrust to the Lord? His entire life. Everything! He knew God would guard his life to the day when Christ comes to reward His church. If you are a true believer, God will protect you in the same way.

GOD'S GUARANTEE

The Greek word for *keep* in the verse 1 of Jude refers not only to a watchful guard, but also to a guarantee. When you were saved, God gave you the Holy Spirit as a guarantee that someday you would be glorified in His presence. Paul spoke about that in Ephesians 1:13–14:

> Having also believed, you were sealed in Him with the
> Holy Spirit of promise, who is given as a pledge of our
> inheritance, with a view to the redemption of God's
> own possession, to the praise of His glory.

The Greek word for "pledge" (*arrabōn*) means "down payment." We know God won't renege on His promises to us because He has given us the Holy Spirit as a down payment on them. God provided our guarantee because He knows we need to have confidence in our salvation. We have not yet been totally redeemed. We have been redeemed spiritually, but we await the redemption of our bodies (Rom. 8:23). We haven't received our full inheritance because we're not in heaven. But we know it will certainly happen one day because the indwelling Holy Spirit guarantees it.

A form of *arrabōn* also came to be used for an engagement ring. The Bible tells us that one day there will be a marriage supper where Christ is the Bridegroom and the church is the bride (Rev. 19:7–10). He gave the church an engagement ring—a symbol of commitment. The Holy Spirit is that engagement ring. He represents God's commitment and investment in us. Your future glory is guaranteed by God Himself.

GOD'S POWER

Because they were living in the midst of apostasy and wickedness, the believers to whom Jude wrote were undoubtedly thinking, *Am I in danger of being overcome by such evil? Will I be safe in the midst of apostasy? Will I be able to remain in the sphere of God's blessing? Can I avoid contamination?*

What was Jude's response? Did he warn them that demons can be transferred or inherited? Did he tell them to avoid danger by rebuking Satan or binding the demons of apostasy and wickedness? No. In stark contrast to all that, he assured them with this great benediction:

> To Him [Christ] who is able to keep you from stumbling, and to make you stand in the presence of His glory blameless with great joy, to the only God our Savior, through Jesus Christ our Lord, be glory, majesty, dominion and authority, before all time and now and forever. (vv. 24–25)

We are secure in God's power no matter what the armies of hell throw against us. Notice that Jude focused the believers' attention on God and His power, not on Satan and demons. Why? Because only God has the power to keep us from falling and present us in Christlike purity before Himself. The confidence that He will keep that promise is the most effective helmet we can wear into the spiritual battle.

THE SWORD
OF THE SPIRIT

crx

Vera Kadaeva, a believer in Moscow, wrote this account about her life during the coup d'état attempt against former Soviet president Mikhail Gorbachev:

> At 8:00 in the morning, we were informed about what happened the night before. My first thought was "Lord! How little we managed to do for You!" The desire to tell people about Christ arose. A prayer sounded in my heart, "Lord! Teach me to do Your will."
>
> During the day I saw tanks and armored cars on the streets of Moscow; the city was raged and agitated. Crowds of people walked toward the building of the Russian Parliament.
>
> During the evening service, the church celebrated the bright holiday of our Lord's Transfiguration. I sat in the church and felt uneasy. Because this could possibly

be my last opportunity, I decided to take some Gospels, magazines, and brochures ... and talk to people about Christ....

The Manezhnaya Square was filled with people: visitors, foreigners, and children. On the square were tanks, armored cars, and a circle of soldiers with machine guns. I got an idea of taking the Gospel in my hands and going toward the tanks through the circle of soldiers. Nobody even paid attention to me. I gave the Gospels to the soldiers. Soldiers and officers of ordinary and special militia who surrounded the square jumped off the tanks and approached me. I only saw their faces and hands. Even now they stand before my eyes. One soldier said, "Give me the book about God, too." ...

On the Tverskiy Boulevard, a whole group of armored cars stopped. We got out of the car and started to distribute Gospels among the soldiers saying the word again and again, "You shall not kill!" The action of these words was like that of an electrical shock. Soldiers shuddered when they heard the Word of God. One soldier's eyes even started to water....

At noon we got to the building of the Russian Parliament.... Here, the defenders of the Parliament remained a third day. It rained heavily. We walked through the puddles and mud carrying Gospels in our hands distributing them among the soldiers of the tank crews who took President Yeltsin's side....

I started across the square, which is now called Free Russian Square, toward the barricades on Kalinin Avenue. The pedestrian part was all dug up by bulldozers. Pieces of reinforced concrete and fittings were piled high. Barricades made of trolley-cars and trucks turned sideways blocked the highways.... People were hiding from the rain in trolley-cars. Behind the trolley-cars was a human barrier of people clasping hands and standing shoulder to shoulder. Behind them, tanks and armored cars blocked the avenue.

> Nobody was able to break through the barricade
> from either side. I asked them to let me pass and dis-
> tribute Gospels among the soldiers. In my hands I held
> a Gospel with the cross on the cover. They unclasped
> their hands and I squeezed between the tanks.
>
> A soldier hurried toward me. I said, "Brother, take
> a Gospel!" He looked at me with wide open eyes.
> "Really?" He grabbed it with dirty hands and put it
> inside his coat. Then, as an afterthought, he said,
> "Give me three more. For friends!"
>
> Thus, giving away Gospels, I could get to the
> other side of the barricades. There was no fear. It felt
> like my feet weren't touching the ground. There was
> great joy because I carried the Word of God which is
> God's power for salvation to every believer.... With the
> Gospel, it was possible to pass through the barricades.
> There are no bounds for the Word of God.[1]

There are no bounds for the Word of God because it is a divinely powerful, spiritually effective weapon. In Ephesians 6:17 Paul called it "the sword of the Spirit." The Greek word he used refers to a dagger anywhere from six to eighteen inches long. It was carried in a sheath or scabbard at the soldier's side and used in hand-to-hand combat.

The sword of the Spirit, therefore, is not a broadsword that you just flail around, hoping to do some damage. It is incisive; it must hit a vulnerable spot, or it won't be effective.

ITS QUALITIES

In verse 17, Paul defined the sword of the Spirit as "the word of God." That means we have a divine sword with certain inherent qualities. What are they?

First, God's Word is infallible. The Bible in its entirety has no mistakes. It is faultless, flawless, and without blemish because it was written by God, whose character has no blemishes. According to Psalm 19:7, "The law of the LORD is perfect."

The Bible is also inerrant. It contains no factual errors, historical fallacies, scientific blunders, or spiritual delusions. It is perfect in every jot and tittle. According to Proverbs 30:5, "*Every* word of God is tested." That means every word is pure and true. The Bible is the only book that never makes a mistake—everything it says is the truth.

The Bible tells us the absolute truth about life and death, time and eternity, heaven and hell, right and wrong, men and women, old people and young people. It gives us the truth about children, about society, and about every relationship between God and man, man and man, and man and nature. It is the truth about everything that's needful.

Another quality is the Word's completeness. Nothing needs to be added to or taken away from it. Today some people claim to be receiving further revelation, but by adding to the Word they are implying, either directly or indirectly, that it is not complete. Proverbs 30:6 tells them this: "Do not add to His words or He will reprove you, and you will be proved a liar."

God's Word is also authoritative. As the divine author of the Bible, God is the final authority. Isaiah said, "Listen, O heavens, and hear, O earth; for the Lord speaks" (1:2). When God speaks, we should listen.

Because His Word is authoritative, we are to obey it. Christ said, "You are My friends if you do what I command you" (John 15:14). Obedience is a mark of a true follower of Christ. In Galatians 3:10 Paul said, "Cursed is everyone who does not abide by all things written in the Book of the Law, to perform them."

God's Word is also sufficient. In 2 Timothy 3:16–17 Paul said, "All Scripture is inspired by God and profitable for teaching, for reproof, for correction, for training in righteousness; *so that the man of God may be adequate, equipped for every good work.*" The Word instructs believers in what is right, rebukes them when they do wrong, and shows them how to walk in the right path. It equips them for every good work. It is utterly sufficient. There is no other source of necessary spiritual truth.

Another quality is the Word's effectiveness. When the Bible speaks, things happen. The Word transforms lives. In Isaiah 55:11, the Lord gave this promise: "My word ... will not return to Me empty, without accomplishing what I desire, and without succeeding in the matter for which I sent it."

Still another quality is that God's Word is determinative. A person's response to the Word reveals his or her relationship to God. Jesus said to a rebellious audience, "He who is of God hears [obeys] the words of God; for this reason you do not hear them, because you are not of God" (John 8:47). If obedience to God's Word is the pattern of your life, it reveals you belong to God. Conversely, if you are perpetually disobeying God's Word, it shows that you do not belong to Him. In that sense, the Bible becomes a determiner of a person's eternal destiny and relationship with God.

When engaged in battle against Satan and his army, you can be confident of the divine quality of your sword. It has been well said that the Bible is an armory of heavenly weapons, a laboratory of infallible medicines, a mine of exhaustless wealth, a guidebook for every road, a chart for every sea, a medicine for every malady, and a balm for every wound.

God's Word is a divinely powerful weapon. If you don't use it on the battlefield, you'll quickly become disabled.

Its Invincibility

God's Word is described as the sword "of the Spirit." That phrase can be translated "spiritual." The sword is spiritual in the sense that the weapons of our warfare are not man made (2 Cor. 10:4). Fighting spiritual wickedness calls for spiritual weapons. All our weapons—the belt, breastplate, shoes, shield, and helmet—are spiritual.

The phrase can also refer to a sword that is given by the Spirit. That speaks of where the sword comes from. Putting the two thoughts together gives the idea that our sword is spiritual because it was given to us by the Holy Spirit. That makes God's Word a unique weapon, for it was not forged on human anvils or tempered in earthly fires. Rather it has a divine origin, so nothing can overpower it. Any earthly sword pales in light of the invincibility of God's Word in the hand of a knowledgeable, righteous saint.

When you become a Christian, you receive the sword in the form of the Bible. An unbeliever might have the Bible, but he doesn't have within him the resident truth Teacher, the Holy Spirit, who makes the Bible meaningful. That's why he doesn't understand the things of God (1 Cor. 2:14). Christ said, "The Helper, the Holy Spirit, whom the Father will send in My name, He will teach you [believers] all things" (John 14:26). The Spirit of God indwells the believer and enlightens his or her understanding of what the Word teaches.

When you wield your sword with understanding, people will be saved, "for it is the power of God for salvation" (Rom. 1:16). God uses His Word to cut a swath through Satan's dominion and liberate the lost from the kingdom of darkness. According to Hebrews 4:12, the Word is "able to judge the thoughts and intentions of the heart." When you present the Word to others, God's judgment is brought to bear on their lives. The Word opens the hearts of men, sifting the evidence and showing them their sin and guilt before God.

God's Word brings truth to error, happiness to sadness, light to darkness, and growth to stagnation. It's no wonder that David wrote:

> The law of the LORD is perfect, restoring the soul;
> The testimony of the LORD is sure, making wise the
>   simple.
> The precepts of the LORD are right, rejoicing the
>   heart;
> The commandment of the LORD is pure, enlightening
>   the eyes.
> The fear of the LORD is clean, enduring forever;
> The judgments of the LORD are true; they are righ-
>   teous altogether.
> They are more desirable than gold, yes, than much
>   fine gold;
> Sweeter also than honey and the drippings of the
>   honeycomb.
> Moreover, by them Your servant is warned;
> In keeping them there is great reward. (Ps. 19:7–11)

This unique weapon, the sword of the Spirit, can be used both defensively and offensively on the battlefield.

ITS DEFENSIVE USE

By properly using God's Word, you can parry Satan's blows and defend yourself from whatever angle he might attack.

A WRONG EXAMPLE

Apparently the champions of today's spiritual-warfare movement do not believe God's Word is always sufficient to parry the blows of Satan. In their attempt to help so-called believers, these individuals supposedly exorcise demons by entering into extended and bizarre conversations with them. Deliverance sessions can take anywhere from several minutes to many weeks, only to have the demons sometimes come back. Often the deliverer will need to repeat his questions or commands because the demons will not cooperate or obey. The following excerpt is from one of several sessions a professor had with Dottie, a so-called believer:

> Suddenly, in the midst of the session as we spoke of their [the demons'] exposure, they broke in:
> "They don't like you because you tell too much, and you talk too much, and too many people are getting convinced!"
> "Too many are getting convinced of what?" I responded.
> "We have been at war with you for too doggone long, and we are sick of it!"
> "Who is 'we'?" I demanded.
> "What do you mean, 'we'? You know who I am." Anger flared.
> "What is your name?"
> "Oh, come on!" Disgust filled the demon's voice.
> "What is your name?" I insisted.

"You know my name. You named me. You named
me last time I was here. You named me. You named
me. So give me my name back!"

"No, you tell me your name," I persisted.

"Oh, shut up!" came the not-too-polite reply.

"You are under the authority of Jesus Christ. You
are to respect Him and His servants! Now I want you
to confess that you will leave today.... I command you
to leave by the authority of Christ."

"I'll kill her first," he repeated three times. "You
can't stop me from killing her!"

"Yes, I can. I forbid you to do it!"

"How?" He tried to delay.

"Jesus forbids you."

"You can't do that!" he protested.[2]

Can you imagine reading a bizarre account like that in the
Gospels? Dottie's true need was not for the right deliverance technique; rather, the indwelling demons were evidence of her need for
repentance and salvation. Rather than engaging in repartee with
the demons, the professor should have been challenging Dottie
herself with the sword of the Spirit, God's Word.

Those in the spiritual-warfare movement point to Matthew
12:29 in an attempt to support what they do. There Christ said,
"How can anyone enter the strong man's house and carry off his
property, unless he first binds the strong man?"

But Christ wasn't laying down a principle for believers to follow in casting out individual demons. He was simply describing His
own power over Satan because religious leaders had just attributed
His supernatural activity to an alliance with Satan (v. 24). In one
sense Christ bound the strong man. Satan is a defeated foe (Col.
2:15). He has been rendered powerless over us (Heb. 2:14).

Still, Satan's ultimate defeat is in the future. Revelation 20:1–3,
for instance, makes it clear that Satan will be bound during Christ's
earthly reign. When the time for that comes, a single angel will do
the task, not believers (v. 1). Later Satan will be cast into the lake
of fire forever (v. 10). Until then, however, he is on the loose,

prowling "around like a roaring lion, seeking someone to devour" (1 Peter 5:8). Our task is not to bind Satan. We are simply told to resist him (v. 9). If we do that, he will flee (James 4:7).

Another verse commonly misapplied by the spiritual-warfare movement is Matthew 16:19, where Jesus said: "I will give you the keys of the kingdom of heaven; and whatever you bind on earth shall have been bound in heaven, and whatever you loose on earth shall have been loosed in heaven."

In its context that verse refers to approving (binding) or disapproving (loosing) the actions of others, not binding demons. He speaks of church discipline, not demonic warfare. In my commentary I explained the meaning of the verse in this way:

> Shortly after His resurrection, Jesus told the disciples, "If you forgive the sins of any, their sins have been forgiven them; if you retain the sins of any, they have been retained" (John 20:23)....
>
> He then said to the church as a whole what He earlier had said to Peter and the other apostles: "Truly I say to you, whatever you shall bind on earth shall be bound in heaven; and whatever you loose on earth shall be loosed in heaven" (v. 18).
>
> In other words, a duly constituted body of believers has the right to tell an unrepentant brother that he is out of line with God's Word and has no right to fellowship with God's people.
>
> Christians have such authority because they have the truth of God's authoritative Word by which to judge.... Christians can authoritatively declare what is acceptable to God or forbidden by Him because they have His Word.
>
> Christians do not determine what is right and wrong, forgiven and unforgiven. Rather, on the basis of God's Word, they recognize and proclaim what God has already determined to be right or wrong, forgiven or unforgiven. When they judge on the basis of God's Word, they can be certain their judgment corresponds with the judgment of heaven.[3]

THE RIGHT EXAMPLE

Christ's method of dealing with Satan and his minions is a far cry from the bizarre techniques of today's spiritual-warfare movement. When Satan came against Him with three fiery temptations, Christ did not enter into an extended dialogue. Neither did He condemn or bind the Devil. He responded by using the sword of the Spirit (Matt. 4:1–11).

In the first temptation Satan told Christ, "Turn the stones into bread. Don't wait for God to supply Your needs. Take the initiative and grab what You want" (see v. 3). Christ responded by quoting Deuteronomy 8:3, which related exactly to that temptation.

In the second temptation Satan said, "Dive off the temple and let God catch You" (see Matt. 4:6). Satan was urging Christ to put God's promise to a test. Christ parried that blow with razor-sharp precision by quoting Deuteronomy 6:16.

Satan tempted Christ the third time by offering Him right then what He would have to suffer on the cross to gain later on (Matt. 4:9). Again Christ responded with a precise use of Scripture (Deut. 6:13).

When Christ resisted Satan by using God's Word, what happened? The Devil left.

What can we learn from Christ's example? That we need to apply the specifics of God's Word to the specifics of the temptation. Using the sword of the Spirit is much more than merely owning a Bible; it is knowing the specific scriptural principle that applies to the specific temptation.

Let me illustrate that point in this way: In Romans 10:17, Paul said, "Faith comes from hearing, and hearing by the word of Christ." The term translated "word" here is the same one used in Ephesians 6:17. He speaks of a specific statement of Scripture, not the broad entirety of Scripture. Saving faith doesn't come from hearing just any part of the Word. Faith comes by hearing specific truths about Christ's life, death, burial, and resurrection. It comes by hearing specific challenges that convict us of our own sin and need. Similarly, when Satan confronts you with temptation or false teaching, you need to respond with verses that specifically address whatever he's troubling you with. It won't do any good just to wave a Bible in front of him. Use the sword as an instrument of precision.

For example, if I am tempted to be discouraged, I think of verses that relate to that problem. A man asked me, "What Bible verses do you use when you become sorrowful? What Bible verses do you use when you want to renew your commitment?" He was asking the right questions.

On the other hand, you could own a Bible warehouse but not have the sword of the Spirit. There are Christians who have sat in churches and Bible classes for years but don't know the principles for stopping the simplest attack. Satan will find out an area where you don't know the biblical principles, and that's where he'll start his attack.

The only way you will know victory in the Christian life is by daily studying the principles of God's Word. That way you'll be ready to apply them whenever the world, the flesh, and the Devil choose to attack. That means you must saturate your mind with God's Word.

The reason so many Christians fall to temptation is they just don't know how Scripture deals with what's troubling them. They aren't equipped to use the sword properly. It's tragic for someone to be a Christian a long time and not be able to use the sword properly. You might say, "I've tried, but I don't understand it." But no believer can plead ignorance. God has given us not only His Word, but also the resident truth Teacher, who indwells us. He will enlighten our understanding if we submit to His teachings.

What about you? Do you know how to use God's Word defensively? God's Word is effective, if used the right way.

ITS OFFENSIVE USE

THE POWER OF GOD'S WORD

I'm glad God's Word has both offensive and defensive capabilities because I would hate to fight defensively on the battlefield all the time. I love trying to whack away some of the jungle in Satan's kingdom with my sword. Every time I take the gospel to an unbeliever, I see myself blazing through Satan's dominion. Every time someone is redeemed, I see a swath cut through his dark kingdom.

I love to have opportunities to present God's Word because it attacks Satan's system. Do you realize when you present God's Word by teaching it to your children, talking about it to your friends, or telling other students, you are cutting your way through Satan's kingdom? That's because God's Word "is the power of God for salvation" (Rom. 1:16).

Tragically, many advocates of today's spiritual-warfare movement take the focus off God's Word and put it on miraculous signs and wonders instead. They end up denigrating the power of Scripture. Pastor John Wimber said:

> Once I accepted the fact that all the spiritual gifts are for today, I found a key for effective evangelism: combining the *proclamation* with the *demonstration* of the gospel.... There is unusual power and effectiveness in this form of evangelism, which is the reason I call it "power evangelism."[4]

In another book he wrote:

> By accepting the supernatural as a natural part of kingdom living, we consciously encounter Satan's kingdom daily. It is here that we must take on Christ's authority, as given in the Great Commission, to heal diseases and cast out demons, to demonstrate God's reign.
>
> These conflicts are called power encounters, the clashing of the kingdom of God with the kingdom of Satan. They may occur in many circumstances, the expulsion of demons being the most dramatic form, although power encounters are far from limited only to the demonic. When unbelievers either have a power encounter or witness one, they are moved to a new level of awareness in making a decision for Christ. Christ is present and they know it. Power encounters are doorways to the kingdom of God.[5]

In an attempt to find biblical support for power evangelism, advocates cite Mark 16:14–18, which reads:

> Afterward He [Christ] appeared to the eleven them-
> selves as they were reclining at the table, and He
> reproached them for their unbelief and hardness of
> heart, because they had not believed those who had
> seen Him after He had risen. And He said to them,
> "Go into all the world and preach the gospel to all
> creation. He who has believed and has been baptized
> shall be saved; but he who has disbelieved shall be
> condemned. "These signs will accompany those who
> have believed: in My name they will cast out
> demons, they will speak with new tongues; they will
> pick up serpents, and if they drink any deadly poison,
> it shall not hurt them; they will lay hands on the
> sick, and they will recover."

But that passage is not a proof text for power evangelism. As we have noted, miraculous signs were unique credentials for the apostles and their gospel message. In their book *The Charismatic Phenomenon* Drs. Peter Masters and John Whitcomb wrote, "These words were *specifically* addressed to the eleven, and therefore no present-day believers need lose their assurance because they cannot heal the sick, triumph over venomous snakes or survive deadly poisons!"[6]

To believe signs and wonders are the key to evangelism is to slight the regenerative work of the Holy Spirit. As Dr. Ken Sarles has pointed out:

> The *real* miracle in conversion is not the *persuasion* of
> the mind by sensationalized evidence, but the *reorienta-*
> *tion* of the mind by the biblical evidence that already
> exists! This reorientation of perspective is a supernatural
> work accomplished only by the Holy Spirit in regenera-
> tion. What is needed is not new *objects* to see (signs and

wonders) but new *eyes* with which to see (regeneration)
the object that is already there (the testimony of
Scripture).[7]

Proponents of the modern-day signs and wonders fail to
acknowledge the purpose of miracles in the early church.
Miraculous gifts were inextricably bound to the ministry of the
apostles. We know there are no apostles today because Scripture
says two of the apostolic credentials were being an eyewitness of the
resurrected Christ (Acts 1:21–23; 1 Cor. 9:1) and having been personally taught divine truth by Christ (Gal. 1:11–12; 1 Cor. 15:3).
Who today can claim such credentials? Who has physically seen the
Lord and been taught by Him? Charles Hodge commented:

> The signs of an apostle were the insignia of the apos-
> tleship; those things which by divine appointment were
> made the evidence of a mission from God. When these
> were present an obligation rested on all who witnessed
> them to acknowledge the authority of those who bore
> those insignia. When they were absent, it was, on the
> one hand, an act of sacrilege to claim the apostleship;
> and, on the other, an act of apostasy from God to
> admit its possession. To acknowledge the claims of
> those who said they were apostles and were not, was
> (and is) to turn from God to the creature, to receive as
> divine what was in fact human or Satanic.[8]

In Ephesians 2:20, Paul said the church is "built upon the foundation of the apostles and prophets, Christ Jesus Himself being the
corner stone." To claim that believers today exert the same apostolic authority is an attempt to rebuild the church and lay again the
foundation that Christ already established forever.

Moreover, power encounters are not doorways to the kingdom
of God. The teaching of Scripture is opposite to that assertion. In
Matthew 11:20, for example, Christ "began to denounce the cities
in which most of His miracles were done, because they did not

repent." Later on, unbelieving religious leaders demanded that Christ give them a sign. But He replied, "An evil and adulterous generation craves for a sign; and yet no sign will be given to it but the sign of Jonah the prophet" (12:39). As Christ hung on the cross, the leaders again sought after a sign, saying in a mocking way, "Let Him now come down from the cross, and we shall believe in Him" (27:42). Fat chance.

If a person turns a deaf ear to God's Word, no miracle will move him or her to trust God. It is the message that God uses in conversion, not the miracle.

What is God's plan for the offensive battle? Not power evangelism, but the powerful Word of God used with great precision.

THE EFFECTIVENESS OF GOD'S WORD

Satan is much more aware of the effectiveness of God's Word than many of the champions of today's spiritual-warfare movement. The Devil will do anything he can to nullify the efforts of those who present the gospel to the lost. That was Christ's point in the parable of the sower and the seed:

> Behold, the sower went out to sow; and as he sowed, some seeds fell beside the road, and the birds came and ate them up. Others fell on the rocky places, where they did not have much soil; and immediately they sprang up, because they had no depth of soil. But when the sun had risen, they were scorched; and because they had no root, they withered away. Others fell among the thorns, and the thorns came up and choked them out. And others fell on the good soil and yielded a crop, some a hundredfold, some sixty, and some thirty. (Matt. 13:3–8)

In verses 18–23, Jesus explained the meaning of this parable. The sower is anyone who proclaims the Word of God. The seed is the Word of God. When you sow seed, you are using your sword.

In verse 8, He said when the seed finds good ground—when the seed finds a receptive heart—it will bear fruit.

Satan knows God's Word is capable of bearing fruit, so he is busy trying to make sure it doesn't. How? One way is attacking through demons. In verse 4, Jesus said that birds devoured the seed that fell beside the road. That refers to Satan's demonic hosts. Somehow they are able to snatch the Word away so that a person will forget what he or she has heard. Perhaps you remember talking to someone about the Word, but then when you see him or her again, it's as if you never said anything about it. Satan snatches it out of the mind.

Satan also attacks through tribulation. In verse 5, Jesus said some of the seed fell on stony places. It sprang up for a little while, but there was not much earth. As soon as the sun came up, it burned the plant because it had no root, and it withered away (v. 6). It couldn't take the heat. You may have had someone respond positively to your gospel presentation, but then when trials come, the person says, "God, You're not so good after all!" You see him or her walk away from the truth under the pressure of persecution or tribulation.

How else does Satan attack? Through worldliness. In verse 7, Jesus said some of the seed fell among thorns that sprang up and choked it. That refers to people who believe for a little while but are unwilling to say no to the system (v. 22). Because they want the world, they walk away from the Word.

Satan is busy twisting people's perspective of the world, persecuting them, or snatching the Word away, so they won't remember it. He wants to stop the sowing of the seed because he knows it will produce fruit in good soil.

If I didn't believe the Word of God would produce, I would quit preaching and do something else. It is reassuring to know that when we present the Word of God, it will always accomplish what it should (Isa. 55:11).

What is the right way to use God's Word? This striking illustration comes to mind:

A person described three things he saw in a garden among the plants and flowers.

The first was a butterfly that alighted on an attractive flower. It sat for a second or two, then moved on to another, seeing and touching many lovely blossoms but deriving no benefit from them.

Next came a botanist with a large notebook and microscope. He spent some time over each flower and plant, making copious notes of each. But when he had finished, his knowledge was shut away in his notebook; very little of it remained with him.

Then a bee came along, entering a flower here and there and spending time in each, emerging from each blossom laden with pollen. It went in empty and came out full.

There are those who read the Bible, flitting from one favorite passage to another, but getting little from their reading. Others really study and take notes but do not apply the teachings of Scripture. Others—like the bee—spend time over the Word, reading, marking, and inwardly digesting and applying it. Their minds are filled with wisdom and their lives with heavenly sweetness.

Which are you? A butterfly, flitting from class to class, Bible study to Bible study, seminar to seminar, book to book, flapping your pretty wings but never changing? A botanist—with enough notebooks to sink a small battleship? Or are you a bee coming in empty and going out full, turning your knowledge into the honey that makes life sweet?

PRAYERS ON THE BATTLEGROUND

ᴄ·ᴧ

Atechnique of today's spiritual-warfare movement is "warfare praying." That speaks of confrontation with Satan and demons during prayer. A pastor explained it in this way:

> In a prayer of rebuke we break demons' hold on a person, contain their power, and eliminate their presence.... I usually say, "In the name of Jesus, I rebuke you, evil spirit. You have no part in Jane's life."[1]

What about that prayer of rebuke? Is it biblical? Think of it in this way: Whom is it addressed to? Not God, but a demon. By definition, that's not even prayer! Furthermore, believers are not supposed to try to control demons. As we noted before, God sometimes allows demons to afflict believers *externally* for His own sovereign purposes. Like Paul, who was afflicted with a demon who buffeted him, we are to pray *to God*, not to the demon. And we must be prepared to submit to God's sovereign plan, even if that means we're still under attack. God's sufficient grace can enable us, like Paul, to grow spiritually in our afflictions. And God promises us the power to resist temptation (1 Cor. 10:13).

Another pastor who writes often about spiritual warfare suggested different warfare prayers for his readers. Here's one example:

> In the name of the Lord Jesus Christ I resist all of Satan's
> activity to hold [John Smith] in blindness and darkness.
> Exercising my authority which is given to me in my union
> with the Lord Jesus Christ, I pull down the strongholds
> which the kingdom of darkness has formed against
> [John]. I smash and break and destroy all those plans
> formed against [John's] mind, his will, his emotions, and
> his body. I destroy in prayer the spiritual blindness and
> deafness that Satan keeps upon him.[2]

Who is he kidding? Does he think his words will be more effective than *God's* Word against Satan? After all, only God can remove spiritual blindness. That's why we "do not preach ourselves but Christ Jesus as Lord" (2 Cor. 4:5). Are believers to destroy plans formed against another person's mind, emotions, will, and body? That seems like some kind of telepathic effort. It is certainly not biblical prayer. To pray that God would use His Word to do a spiritual work in a person's life is a far cry from saying, "I resist; I pull down; or I smash, break, and destroy." The truth is, prayers like that have no effect against the powers of darkness.

Later in his book the same author suggested warfare prayers for an adopted child. He believes demons can transfer or pass through generational bloodlines. To prevent that from happening, he encourages parents to have their adopted child say this warfare prayer:

> I cancel out all demonic working that has been
> passed on to me from my ancestors. As one who has
> been crucified with Jesus Christ and raised to walk in

newness of life, I cancel every curse that may have
been put upon me.[3]

But that prayer is neither biblical nor necessary. When any person trusts Christ as Savior and Lord, God cancels or removes all of
Satan's claims against him or her. Paul expressed that thought this
way:

> If God is for us, who is against us? He who did not
> spare His own Son, but delivered Him over for us all,
> how will He not also with Him freely give us all
> things? Who will bring a charge against God's elect?
> God is the one who justifies; who is the one who con-
> demns? Christ Jesus is He who died, yes, rather who
> was raised, who is at the right hand of God, who also
> intercedes for us. (Rom. 8:31–34)

The author suggested another warfare prayer for "the taking
back of ground we may give through our own fleshly or wordly sins":

> I address myself against Satan and all of his kingdom. I
> take away from you and all your powers of darkness
> any ground you are claiming against me when I sinned
> in [name the offense]. I claim that ground back in the
> name of the Lord Jesus Christ. I cover it with the
> blood of the Lord Jesus Christ.[4]

But that's not prayer. Prayer addresses God, not Satan and
demons. Who are we to order around the powers of darkness? *God*
controls them. We don't. The Bible says we are to confess our sins
to God, not talk to the Enemy about them. Also, it is unwitting blas-
phemy to say we can cover anything with Christ's blood. That is not
our prerogative. It is God who chose to cover our sins through
Christ's blood on the cross. Salvation is God's work, not man's.

Victory over Satan and his hosts involves a tremendous commitment to prayer, but there is no biblical basis for special warfare

prayers addressed to the powers of darkness. What is the right way to pray on the battleground? Paul said this:

> With all prayer and petition pray at all times in the
> Spirit, and with this in view, be on the alert with all
> perseverance and petition for all the saints. (Eph. 6:18)

THE NECESSITY OF PRAYER

Over one hundred years ago Charlotte Elliott wrote the hymn "Watch and Pray":

> "Christian, seek not yet repose,"
> Hear thy gracious Savior say;
> Thou art in the midst of foes:
> "Watch and pray."
>
> Principalities and powers,
> Mustering their unseen array,
> Wait for thy unguarded hours:
> "Watch and pray."
>
> Watch, as if on that alone
> Hung the issue of the day;
> Pray, that help may be sent down:
> "Watch and pray."

Why is it necessary to watch and pray? Because prayer works in concert with your spiritual armor. Paul was not saying that in addition to the armor, add prayer; he was implying that prayer is woven into the armor. As we put on the full armor, we are to be engaged in prayer. All through the procedure of arming ourselves and undergoing the demands of the battle, we are to be engaged in prayer.

But prayer is more than an additional weapon; it is the atmosphere in which all our fighting occurs. A lack of prayer will make you prone to faint, grow weary, or abandon the fight when the battle gets hot and heavy.

Paul emphasized the importance of prayer in the book of Ephesians. Probably more than any other book in the Bible, it presents the resources that are ours in Christ. In doing so, it lifts us to great heights. In the beginning of the book we start in the heavenlies, and we stay there until we come to Ephesians 6:18. It is here that God demands we fall on our knees.

You might think, in a book describing such tremendous resources, prayer wouldn't be that necessary. What would we pray for? After all, Paul wrote that we are loved, forgiven, abounding in wisdom, members of God's intimate family, recipients of spiritual gifts, and so much more. In 1:3, Paul said we are blessed "with every spiritual blessing in the heavenly places in Christ." That's a tremendous picture! And it all belongs to the believer.

So why is prayer necessary? Because it is the key to appropriating your resources in Christ. Realize that spiritual armor or any other resource is neither mechanical nor magical. It must be infused with divine power and energy.

Prayer is also necessary because it is the key to depending on God. When you recognize your exalted position and resources in Christ, immediately you face a problem. You might call it doctrinal egoism—a problem defined in 1 Corinthians 10:12: "Let him who thinks he stands take heed that he does not fall." You can become what I call a spiritual atheist: You believe in God but live as though you don't need Him.

Experiencing much success and little failure makes it easy to forget God and believe you are self-sufficient. A passionate, earnest prayer life cannot thrive in such an environment. To remedy that, Richard Baxter offered this counsel:

> Labour hard with your hearts all the while to keep them
> in a reverent, serious, fervent frame, and suffer them not
> to grow remiss and cold, to turn prayer into lip-labour,
> and in lifeless formality ... when the heart is senseless,
> though the voice be earnest. The heart will easily grow
> dull, and customary, and hypocritical, if it be not carefully watched, and diligently followed and stirred up.[5]

THE VARIETY OF PRAYER

In Ephesians 6:18, Paul said we are to pray "with all prayer and petition." "All" refers to all kinds of prayers. "Prayer and petition" includes both general and specific requests.

There are different ways to pray. Some people think the only way to pray is on your knees. Some think the only way you can pray is with your hands up. Others think you must have your hands folded. Some people think you have to pray out of a prayer book. But if you are going to pray all the time, you will have to pray in different ways because you will never be in the same position all day.

You can pray in public or private, with loud cries or quiet whispers. It can be deliberate or spontaneous. There can be prayers of request, thanksgiving, confession, and praise. You can be kneeling, standing, lifting up your hands, or lying prostrate. There is no situation in which you can't pray.

THE FREQUENCY OF PRAYER

In Ephesians 6:18, Paul also said to pray "at all times." There is to be a constant character to prayer. Now obviously you can't carry a little book around and read prayers all day. In Israel you can see many Jewish people going through prayers hour after hour in front of the Wailing Wall. But praying at all times has nothing to do with formulas and repetition; it is simply living your life in the presence of God and with an attitude of God consciousness. Your whole life should rise before God in communion.

I find very few times when I'm not conscious of God. Everything I see and experience in my life simply becomes a prayer. If I experience something good, my first thought is: *God, You're the source of every good and perfect gift. I thank You for that.* If I see something evil, I pray that God will make it right. If I have an opportunity to meet someone who doesn't know Christ, my first response is: "God, it's so sad that person doesn't know You. Draw him [or her] to Yourself." If I see trouble, I pray, "God, You're the Deliverer."

Your prayer life is the truest monitor of how deep your relationship to God is. Martyn Lloyd-Jones said:

> The ultimate test of my understanding of the scriptural teaching is the amount of time I spend in prayer. As theology is ultimately the knowledge of God, the more theology I know, the more it should drive me to seek to know God. Not to know "about" Him but to know Him! The whole object of salvation is to bring me to a knowledge of God.... If all my knowledge does not lead me to prayer there is something wrong somewhere.[6]

The apostle John wrote, "What we have seen and heard we proclaim to you also, so that you too may have fellowship with us; and indeed our fellowship is with the Father, and with His Son Jesus Christ" (1 John 1:3). God wants your fellowship, and prayer is perhaps the greatest expression of it here on earth.

When is the best time to pray? All times. David said, "Evening, and morning, and at noon, will I pray" (Ps. 55:17 KJV). Luke said, Jesus "went off to the mountain to pray, and He spent the whole night in prayer to God" (6:12). Christian soldiers are to pray at all times so that whenever the battle starts, they are ready. Their whole life is opened totally to God.

THE POWER OF PRAYER

We are to pray "in the Spirit" (Eph. 6:18). That means making your own prayers consistent with the mind and will of the Spirit, who "helps our weakness; for we do not know how to pray as we should, but the Spirit Himself intercedes for us with groanings too deep for words; and He who searches the hearts knows what the mind of the Spirit is, because He intercedes for the saints according to the will of God" (Rom. 8:26–27).

How do we pray in concert with the Spirit? By being filled with the Spirit. That is the same as being filled with God's Word (Eph.

5:18–20; cf. Col. 3:16–17). It is allowing God's Word to infuse every part of your being. If you want to be Spirit filled, feed yourself a steady diet of God's Word. That's how the Holy Spirit harmonizes your will and prayers with His.

THE MANNER OF PRAYER

VIGILANT PRAYER

In Ephesians 6:18, Paul said to "be on the alert with all perseverance and petition." Christ Himself emphasized the importance of vigilance in prayer, for shortly before He was arrested,

> He took with Him Peter and the two sons of Zebedee, and began to be grieved and distressed. Then He said to them, "My soul is deeply grieved, to the point of death; remain here and keep watch with Me."
> And He went a little beyond them, and fell on His face and prayed, saying, "My Father, if it is possible, let this cup pass from Me; yet not as I will, but as You will." (Matt. 26:37–39)

Christ's mission was to suffer and die for the sins of the world. Although unable to sin, He could nevertheless experience the full fury of temptation (Heb. 4:15). He had already experienced distress over humanity's sin, but now His anguish became more intense as His crucifixion drew near. He, the spotless Son of God, was repulsed over the prospect of taking upon Himself the full magnitude and defilement of humanity's sin. He would experience the ultimate loneliness of being forsaken by His Father as He became sin for us. The agony of this temptation was so great that it would have been enough to kill Him.

Although Satan is not mentioned by name in this account, he undoubtedly tempted Christ to demand His divine rights. Perhaps he suggested, "Why should the Author of Justice subject Himself to the grossest injustice? Why should the Creator of life submit to death?" We can be sure Satan was calling for Christ to disobey His Father by avoiding the cross. Why? Because Satan wanted to prevent the work of salvation.

Notice that Christ did not confront Satan or enter into warfare prayers. Although anticipating the cross was excruciating, Christ submissively prayed, "Not as I will, but as You will" (Matt. 26:39).

When Christ returned to the three disciples, He found them sleeping and said, "You men could not keep watch with Me for one hour? Keep watching and praying that you may not enter into temptation; the spirit is willing, but the flesh is weak" (vv. 40–41).

He was warning them not to rely on their own power to overcome Satan. Instead of fighting the Devil head-on, they were to approach God in prayer. But in this case, the disciples fell asleep instead of keeping watch.

What can we learn from Christ's example of prayer? First, since the very Son of God needed to pray in the midst of temptation, how much more do we? Second, prayer is not a means of bending God's will to our own, but of submitting our will to His. If Christ submitted to the Father's will, how much more should we.

PERSISTENT PRAYER

We are to be not only vigilant in prayer but also persistent. In Ephesians 6:18, Paul said, "Be on the alert with all perseverance." The Greek word for "perseverance" speaks of steadfastness. Prayer is more than free and easy communication with the Lord, but a life of persevering. That was illustrated in Christ's parable about an unjust judge (Luke 18:1–8). A woman kept coming and begging before the judge. Finally, he did what she wanted. We too need to demonstrate to the Lord that we really care about what we're asking for. If you *really* want what you're praying for, persistence in prayer will come naturally.

In another parable Christ spoke of a man who kept banging on the door of a friend for some food (Luke 11:5–10). The friend said, "Do not bother me. My wife and children are already in bed. I'm not getting up." But the man kept banging until the friend got up and gave him the bread.

In both stories the woman and the hungry man kept persisting until they received what they were asking for. Similarly, we should be faithful and persistent in our prayers, knowing "that we may receive mercy and find grace to help in time of need" (Heb. 4:16).

SPECIFIC PRAYER

The believer is also to pray specifically. In Ephesians 6:18, Paul said, "Be on the alert with all perseverance and petition." The Greek word for "petition" refers to specific requests. Why should you pray specifically? Because God answers prayer to display His power. If you don't pray specifically, you won't see God at work.

When she was little, my daughter Marcy used to pray, "God bless the whole wide world." I would say, "Marcy, honey, you can't pray that way. He won't make the whole world feel better. That's too general; you need to pray about specifics." She learned how to do that. When you pray specifically, you will see God answer specifically for His glory.

Our specific requests should focus on spiritual issues. Praying for physical needs—praying for someone's rheumatism, heart problems, broken leg, or surgery—is important. I pray for people's physical needs, but more than that I pray that God will give the believer victory in battle against the Enemy. That was Paul's primary focus in Ephesians 6:18. One saint prayed for victory in battle in this way:

O Lord,

I bless thee that the issue of the battle between thyself
    and Satan
    has never been uncertain,
    and will end in victory.

Calvary broke the dragon's head,
    and I contend with a vanquished foe,
    who with all his subtlety and strength
    has already been overcome.

When I feel the serpent at my heel
    may I remember him whose heel was bruised,
    but who, when bruised, broke the devil's head.

My soul with inward joy extols the mighty conqueror.

Heal me of any wounds received in the great conflict;
    if I have gathered defilement,
    if my faith has suffered damage,
    if my hope is less than bright,
    if my love is not fervent,
    if some creature-comfort occupies my heart,
    if my soul sinks under the pressure of the fight.

O thou whose every promise is balm,
    every touch life,
    draw near to thy weary warrior,
    refresh me, that I may rise again to wage the strife,
    and never tire until my enemy is trodden down.

Give me such fellowship with thee that I may defy
    Satan,
    unbelief, the flesh, the world,
    with delight that comes not from a creature,
    and which a creature cannot mar.

Give me a draught of the eternal fountain
    that lieth in thy immutable, everlasting love and
    decree.

Then shall my hand never weaken, my feet never stumble,
    my sword never rest, my shield never rust,
    my helmet never shatter, my breastplate never fall,
    my strength rests in the power of thy might.[7]

THE OBJECTS OF PRAYER

Who are we to pray for? "All the saints" (Eph. 6:18). We are to pray for one another. Notice that Satan and demons are not the objects of biblical prayer. We are not told to say, "I address myself against Satan and all his kingdom." We are not told to demand the return of lost ground. We are not told to say, "I rebuke you, evil spirit." We are not told to destroy spiritual blindness. Such bizarre techniques have no place in spiritual warfare.

What are we to do? Pray for others. Doing so is vital to the health of the church body. When one part of your body suffers, the rest of your body compensates to help strengthen it. Similarly, when a member of the church body is weak or wounded, we should pray for him or her.

As a side effect, praying for the spiritual health of others is beneficial for you as well. Dr. Lloyd-Jones made this observation:

> Before the outbreak of the Spanish Civil War, in Barcelona, Madrid and other places, there were psychological clinics with large numbers of neurotics undergoing drug treatment and others attending regularly for psychoanalysis and such like. They had their personal problems, their worries, their anxieties, their temptations, having to go back week after week, month after month, to the clinics in order to be kept going.
>
> Then came the Civil War; and one of the first and most striking effects of that War was that it virtually emptied the psychological and psychiatric clinics. These neurotic people were suddenly cured by a greater anxiety, the anxiety about their whole position, whether their homes would still be there, whether their husbands would still be alive, whether their children would be killed. The greater anxieties got rid of the lesser ones. In having to give attention to the bigger problem they forgot their own personal and somewhat petty problems.[8]

Do you want to be a spiritually healthy person? Then lose yourself in the things that matter. Lose yourself in consuming prayer for the kingdom of God, and you won't be troubled by your lesser anxieties.

Lloyd-Jones continued:

> A greater fear drives out lesser fears; and I am applying that principle to this whole question of prayer. When you feel that you are in a kind of vortex, and you cannot forget yourself; when you are sorry for yourself and feeling that you are having an unusually hard time with everything against you and [it's] almost enough to drive you to despair, one of the best remedies is to sit down and say, "What about so-and-so? What about this person, what about that person, what about Christians in other countries?" Get down on your knees and pray for them, and you will soon get up finding that you have forgotten yourself.... You will find that in praying for them you are solving your own problems and obtaining release.[9]

It is wonderful to pray for others, but you cannot do so effectively unless you know what is going on in their lives. You know your own problems very well, but that's not where you need to spend the bulk of your prayer time. Be praying for other people, watching for their needs. Selfishness kills that perspective. Most of us never get serious about prayer until some trouble occurs in our own lives. We are often ten times more intense about our own problems than we are about anyone else's. That reveals our self-centeredness.

What about the people around you? Are you aware of their spiritual needs? Are you praying for your spouse, children, friends, neighbors, and people in your Bible study? Or do you neglect them?

Prayer requires that we communicate with one another, so we'll know what to pray about. That's the example Paul gave to the Ephesian church:

Pray on my behalf, that utterance may be given to me in the opening of my mouth, to make known with boldness the mystery of the gospel, for which I am an ambassador in chains; that in proclaiming it I may speak boldly, as I ought to speak.

But that you also may know about my circumstances, how I am doing, Tychicus, the beloved brother and faithful minister in the Lord, will make everything known to you. I have sent him to you for this very purpose, so that you may know about us, and that he may comfort your hearts. (Eph. 6:19–22)

Since Paul didn't expect the Ephesians to pray for him without some information, he brought word to them through his good friend Tychicus. What did Paul want them to pray for? That a spiritual battle might be won. He was a prisoner in Rome and wanted to have courage in speaking about Christ. God answered that prayer. We know from the book of Philippians that his gospel witness became "well known throughout the whole praetorian guard and to everyone else" (1:13). His courage helped other believers speak the Word of God fearlessly (v. 14).

Is prayer woven into your spiritual armor? In his book *Knowing God*, J. I. Packer wrote:

We must learn to measure ourselves, not by our knowledge about God, not by our gifts and responsibilities in the church, but by how we pray and what goes on in our hearts. Many of us, I suspect, have no idea how impoverished we are at this level. Let us ask the Lord to show us.[10]

THE COMMANDS
FOR VICTORY

ᥴᨠ

General Norman Schwarzkopf, former commander of the United States Central Command and the architect of Operation Desert Storm, said:

> I really think of myself as a soldier who tries to do his duty with honor, serving his country. Contrary to what has been said about me, I have never had any illusions of grandeur, of leading huge armies into battle, and I will confess that sometimes the awesome responsibility that is placed on my soldier flat scares me to death. But I do recognize that is what I have been trained for, and that's what the United States has a professional military for, and certainly a crisis is not the time for me to be weak of heart or timid about my responsibilities. All I can do is my best, and when this is all over if I can still say to myself that I did my very best, then that is what is really important to me.[1]

As believers we should do our best to serve and honor Christ, who is our Commander in Chief. By His death, burial, and resurrection, He has won the victory for every believer. Christ came to earth as a man "that through death He might render powerless him who had the power of death, that is, the devil, and might free those who through fear of death were subject to slavery all their lives" (Heb. 2:14–15).

Until our ultimate victory is fully realized in glory, however, Satan and his army will continue to assault the work that God is attempting to accomplish in the lives of His children. That means you can count on facing everyday battles and skirmishes.

How are we to respond to Satan's attacks? Not by using the bizarre methods many today are advocating. Instead, Paul gave these five commands: "Be on the alert, stand firm in the faith, act like men, be strong. Let all that you do be done in love" (1 Cor. 16:13–14).

Those brief commands capsulize the believer's responsibility in spiritual warfare. By obeying them you will do away with your doubts, rise above your sins, supersede your indifferences, and walk worthy of your heavenly calling. In short, it's the way to do your best for Christ. Let's take a closer look at each command.

BE ALERT

More than sixty years ago the following drama acted itself out in the Pacific:

> In the middle of the night, Lt. Hirata Matsumura got out of his bunk aboard the aircraft carrier Hiryu ... and pulled on a flying suit. Then he trimmed his nails and cut a lock of hair to leave his family. Up on the flight deck, a Nakajima-97 bomber was waiting for him, an 800-kilo torpedo strapped to its belly. The Zeroes took off first that day, then the bombers, then the torpedo planes. For two hours they flew southward above the clouds. Then patches of blue sky opened over Diamond

Head. Lieutenant Matsumura nosed his plane over—
and roared toward Pearl Harbor.[2]

George Campbell, a twenty-five-year-old petty officer on the
USS *Medusa*, recalled what happened next:

> I had just come up topside and had a cup of coffee in
> my hand and was getting ready to read the paper....
> All of a sudden these planes came in, but we were
> used to that because our own planes were always mak-
> ing mock raids. We took a good look at the planes and
> saw the red-sun emblem and we knew it was the real
> thing.... With the first attack that hit us, we really
> didn't fire back that much. By the time they came
> back a second time, we did put up a few shells. Then
> they made a third attack. By that time we did give
> them a little resistance.... The feeling at the time of
> any attack—I was under a few others in the Pacific—
> was that you don't have time for feelings. But
> afterward you realize it, especially when you look
> around and see what happened.[3]

What happened? On December 7, 1941, the Japanese attack on
Pearl Harbor killed more than two thousand Americans and crip-
pled the Pacific Fleet. Why such a devastating defeat? Because it was
a surprise attack.

In spiritual warfare Satan wants to catch you by surprise that
he might achieve similarly devastating results. That's why you
need to "be on the alert" (1 Cor. 16:13). Make a determined
effort to evaluate what the adversary is doing. That command is
necessary because many believers live the Christian life in a state
of stupor. That's what was happening in the church at Corinth.
Instead of living according to biblical principles, they followed
after the popular philosophies and immoral behavior of their
culture. They therefore forfeited divine joy and blessing for not
knowing and obeying God.

FOR TEMPTATION

The believer needs to be wide awake or else he or she will be vulnerable to Satan's temptations. Satan "prowls around like a roaring lion, seeking someone to devour" (1 Peter 5:8). He is wily and crafty and wants to catch believers in the clever traps he sets. Thomas Brooks wrote in *Precious Remedies against Satan's Devices:*

> Satan hath snares for the wise and snares for the simple;
> snares for hypocrites, and snares for the upright; snares
> for generous souls, and snares for [fearful] souls; snares
> for the rich, and snares for the poor; snares for the aged,
> and snares for youth. Happy are those souls that are not
> taken and held in the snares that he hath laid![4]

How are you to handle Satan's temptations? Not by confronting the Devil and saying, "Satan, I bind you." Not by attending a seminar to learn mystical methods of warfare. We are simply told to resist him (James 4:7). If you do, God promises that Satan will flee.

FOR FALSE TEACHERS

You also need to watch out for false teachers. Remember, Satan is a liar who disguises himself as an angel of light and his servants as ministers of righteousness (2 Cor. 11:13–15). One of the manifestations of his lying intent is the proliferation of false teachers who besiege the gospel and the church. Jesus warned, "False Christs and false prophets will arise and will show great signs and wonders, so as to mislead, if possible, even the elect" (Matt. 24:24).

The sad fact is, however, that they will end up misleading many churchgoers. In Matthew 7:21–23, Jesus said:

> Not everyone who says to Me, "Lord, Lord," will
> enter the kingdom of heaven, but he who does the
> will of My Father who is in heaven will enter. Many
> will say to Me on that day, "Lord, Lord, did we not

prophesy in Your name, and in Your name cast out
demons, and in Your name perform many miracles?"
And then I will declare to them, "I never knew you;
depart from Me, you who practice lawlessness."

What was our Lord saying? That many who think they are
believers really aren't. I believe churches throughout the world
today are full of people who are unbelievers and don't know it.
Some of them even believe they are casting out demons in Jesus'
name. They think all is going well, yet they are deceived. For them,
judgment is going to be one big surprise.

Perhaps Jesus' warning in Matthew 7 has you wondering, *Can
unbelievers really cast out demons and do other signs and wonders?*
There are three possibilities: One is that they do their amazing works
by God's own power. It wouldn't be the first time God has used
unbelievers in such a way. After all He used Balaam, the prophet for
hire, and Caiaphas, the vile high priest, to prophesy His truth.

Another possibility is that these unbelievers who believe they
are preaching, casting out demons, and performing other signs and
wonders are actually deceived by Satan or are part of his strategy to
deceive. Moses gave this instruction to the nation of Israel concern-
ing false prophets who would perform signs and wonders:

> If a prophet or a dreamer of dreams arises among you and
> gives you a sign or a wonder, and the sign or the wonder
> comes true, concerning which he spoke to you, saying,
> "Let us go after other gods (whom you have not known)
> and let us serve them," you shall not listen to the words
> of that prophet or that dreamer of dreams; for the LORD
> your God is testing you to find out if you love the LORD
> your God with all your heart and with all your soul. You
> shall follow the LORD your God and fear Him; and you
> shall keep His commandments, listen to His voice, serve
> Him, and cling to Him. But that prophet or that dreamer
> of dreams shall be put to death, because he has counseled
> rebellion against the LORD your God. (Deut. 13:1–5)

Those signs and wonders were probably energized by Satan. The same can be said about the magicians of Egypt who did tricks in their attempt to copy the miracles of Moses.

Our Lord implied that unbelieving Jewish leaders had cast out demons by Satan's power when He said, "If I by Beelzebub cast out demons, by whom do your sons cast them out?" (Matt. 12:27). In a similar vein the book of Acts describes the activity of a satanic sorcerer (8:9–11) and the unbelieving sons of Sceva who cast out demons (19:13–14). Undoubtedly many today who name Christ and do signs and wonders are in reality empowered by Satan.

Scripture tells us that an emphasis on the miraculous and super-natural will characterize the last days. Satan's deceptive activity will include "all power and signs and false wonders" (2 Thess. 2:9). There will be "spirits of demons, performing signs" (Rev. 16:14). Thomas Ice and Robert Dean have commented:

> When examined in the light of the Scripture, this new spiritual warfare seems closer to fitting the description of the final apostasy during the end times of the church age. In addition, the new spiritual-warfare theology increasingly appears to fit the description of the false religious system headed by the false prophet in the coming tribulation period.
>
> It appears more than likely that Satan and his demons are giving many advocates of the new spiritual warfare the types of "power" experiences they are seeking in order to deceive them. Since these advocates tend to emphasize only the demonic realm (and that from a false perspec-tive), they are open to Satan's attacks in the realm of the flesh and, especially because of lack of discernment, the influence of the world-system and its false teachings.[5]

It is also possible that some who purport to do signs and won-ders are fakes. Their claims of exorcising demons and healing the afflicted are simply false and contrived.

Unbelieving, self-deluded people can say, "We preach, cast out demons, and do mighty works." They can claim that God is working through them. Other people who see them might believe the same thing. But an unbeliever—whether his or her signs and wonders are permitted by God, energized by Satan, or the manifestations of clever chicanery—has no part in Christ's kingdom (Matt. 7:23). That's why Christ wants you to build your life on the solid foundation of obedience to God's Word, not the shifting sands of signs and wonders (vv. 24–27).

Why do you need to watch out for false teachers? Because they use the Word of God but distort its teaching. What they say appears to be biblical yet pulls unwary souls away from the faith.

Demons know that speculations, not facts, must fill people's minds. In C. S. Lewis's satire *The Screwtape Letters* the senior demon Screwtape wrote this letter of instruction to his apprentice demon:

> Your man has been accustomed, ever since he was a boy,
> to having a dozen incompatible philosophies dancing
> about together inside his head. He doesn't think of doc-
> trines as primarily "true" or "false," but as "academic"
> or "practical." ... Jargon, not argument, is your best ally
> in keeping him from the Church.[6]

In reality Satan has used that technique successfully by infiltrating today's colleges, seminaries, churches, and so-called Christian radio and television with so much unsound doctrine.

That's scary because wrong teaching "leads to the ruin of the hearers" (2 Tim. 2:14). The Greek word translated "ruin" means "to overturn" or "subvert." It speaks of total destruction. Peter used the same word in speaking of God's destruction of Sodom and Gomorrah (2 Peter 2:6). False teaching is harmful, not healthy. It doesn't edify; it tears down.

It's no wonder the Bible is replete with warnings against false teachers. Jesus said, "Beware of the false prophets, who come to you in sheep's clothing [wool was the garment of a prophet], but inwardly are ravenous wolves" (Matt. 7:15). John stated, "Even now many antichrists have appeared" (1 John 2:18). Paul warned that seducing spirits are on the loose in the church, teaching demonic doctrines (1 Tim. 4:1).

Since false teaching is on the loose in today's church, it's vital that you examine the foundation of your life. Perhaps you respect Christ and have a religious life. The house you are building might look exactly like the one built on the rock. But if it is built on the sand, it will fall down when judgment comes. I tell you this from my heart: Test yourself to see if you are in the faith (2 Cor. 13:5).

If you are a true believer, how can you protect yourself from the danger of false teachers? By exercising spiritual discernment. Paul said, "Be diligent to present yourself approved to God as a workman who does not need to be ashamed, accurately handling the word of truth" (2 Tim. 2:15). Spiritual discernment flourishes in an environment of intense, faithful Bible study. Only there will you find the principles and truths necessary in discerning between truth and error.

As Paul warned the church leaders at Ephesus about false teachers, his concluding word to them was this: "I commend you to God and to the word of His grace, which is able to build you up and to give you the inheritance among all those who are sanctified" (Acts 20:32). He knew that their careful study of God's Word was essential for protecting the church from error.

If you treat God's Word in a superficial, careless way, you will be prone to accept Satan's lies. Protect yourself from Satan's lies by studying God's Word carefully, diligently, and faithfully.

FOR CHRIST'S RETURN

What else should we be on the alert for? Christ's return. The Corinthians missed their opportunity for victory because they were not guarding their Christian walk. They fell to temptation, apathy, false teachers, and prayerlessness. They were not ready for the Lord's return. They needed to reverse their behavior by waking up—by knowing and applying the principles of God's Word. So do many others in the church today. After all:

The night is almost gone, and the day is near. Therefore
let us lay aside the deeds of darkness and put on the
armor of light. Let us behave properly as in the day, not
in carousing and drunkenness, not in sexual promiscuity
and sensuality, not in strife and jealousy. But put on the
Lord Jesus Christ, and make no provision for the flesh
in regard to its lusts. (Rom. 13:12–14)

We need to be alert because we do not know the day or hour of
Christ's coming (Matt. 25:13). John wrote, "Abide in Him, so that
when He appears, we may have confidence and not shrink away
from Him in shame at His coming" (1 John 2:28). What about you?
Are you ready for our Lord's return?

BE FIRM

We also have a command to "stand firm in the faith" (1 Cor.
16:13). That means being rooted or grounded in God's Word.
Many of the Corinthians were blowing with the breeze. Instead of
holding to the supernatural uniqueness of God's revelation, they
mixed the divine Word of God with human philosophies. They held
adulterated teaching on an equal basis with the pure Word and
dragged it into the church.

That's great folly because the Bible has no equal. It alone is
inspired by God (2 Tim. 3:16; 2 Peter 1:20–21).

The Corinthians had given themselves over to a mixture of
paganism and Christianity. They allowed the pagan ecstasies and
trances from their cultural religion to infiltrate the church. The situation was so deplorable that people were standing up in the midst
of the service and—supposedly under the inspiration of the Holy
Spirit—cursing Jesus (1 Cor. 12:2–3)! In addition, some of the
Corinthians were denying Christ's resurrection (15:12).

What was Paul's response to the church's wretched condition?
Was it to set up training sessions so the church leaders could learn
to exorcise demons? Was it to bind the territorial demons of pagan
Corinth? No, Paul told them to stand firm in the faith. They needed

to reaffirm the authority of God's Word, the person of Christ, and the resurrection—the great cornerstones of Christianity.

Unfortunately, the hallmark of today's spiritual-warfare movement is to elevate experience above God's Word. For example, one pastor wrote:

> God uses our experiences to show us more fully what he teaches in Scripture, many times toppling or altering elements of our theology.... Some truths in Scripture cannot be understood until we have had certain experiences. I have found this to be the case with healing. Until I began to experience people being healed, I did not understand many of the Scripture passages on healing.[7]

Dr. Ken Sarles responded:

> If theology is authentically biblical, God-ordained experience will enrich it, not alter it, because God cannot contradict Himself. Rather than beginning with a valid interpretation of the Bible and then allowing the Scriptures to interpret his experience, Wimber seems to start with his own experience, which he then allows to inform his understanding of the biblical text.[8]

Archibald Alexander's book *Thoughts on Religious Experience* offers this wise counsel:

> In judging of religious experience it is all-important to keep steadily in view the system of divine truth contained in the Holy Scriptures; otherwise, our experience, as is too often the case, will degenerate into enthusiasm. Many ardent professors seem too readily to take it for granted that all religious feelings must be good. They therefore take no care to discriminate between the genuine and the spurious, the pure gold and the tinsel. Their only concern is about the ardour of their feelings;

not considering that if they are spurious, the more
intense they are, the further will they lead them astray.[9]

The key to being firm is understanding the revealed truths of
God's Word. Make sure you're exposed to sound doctrine.

BE MATURE

One author offered this all-purpose prayer for confronting the
powers of darkness:

> In the name of the Lord Jesus Christ and by the power
> of His blood, I pull down all levels of the stronghold
> of_____. [Choose items from the following list of
> areas of Satan's strongholds that you desire to pull
> down and smash. You may think of other things—the
> list is suggestive, not exhaustive.][10]

The suggested list is a smorgasbord of thirty-two items, including adultery, cursing and vile language, divorce, peer pressure,
pride, and neglect of Bible study and prayer.

Is that how believers are to grow in the Christian life? Does
filling in the blank and repeating a prayer pull down the strongholds of demons? The Corinthians experienced many of the same
problems, but you don't find Paul telling them to use formulaic
techniques like that. He simply commanded them to "act like
men" (1 Cor. 16:13).

He was telling the Corinthians to grow up. Instead of being
mature, many of the Corinthians were fighting and squabbling with
one another, flitting from one false doctrine to another. Paul told
them, "I, brethren, could not speak to you as to spiritual men, but
as to men of flesh, as to infants in Christ. I gave you milk to drink,
not solid food; for you were not yet able to receive it. Indeed, even
now you are not yet able" (3:1–2).

Paul had to deal with the Corinthians as though they were

children. Sibling rivalries sometimes resulted in their taking other believers to court. Even their religious worship was childish, for it was based on emotion rather than sound doctrine.

Because of their immaturity, they could not defend themselves against the onslaughts of Satan. If the Corinthians had grown up, they would have eliminated their squabbles and ineptitude. Their emotions would have given way to obeying the truth of God's Word.

As believers we are expected to be mature spiritually. How? Not by confronting the powers of darkness and supposedly pulling down strongholds of demons. Rather, Peter said to "long for the pure milk of the word, so that by it you may grow in respect to salvation" (1 Peter 2:2).

Many Christians today have only a shallow knowledge of God's Word. Often it's because they trust in personal experiences or feelings as truth or regard personal comfort and success as their priorities in life. It's what I call "Baby Christianity." But Paul said, "We are no longer to be children, tossed here and there by waves and carried about by every wind of doctrine ... but speaking the truth in love, we are to grow up in all aspects into Him who is the head, even Christ" (Eph. 4:14–15).

BE STRONG

Alpha-Omega Energies, which identifies itself as a traveling evangelistic ministry, claims that everyone on the face of this earth needs to be delivered from demons in its book *The Truth in Deliverance:*

> Who needs deliverance? Anyone in the lineage of Adam has inherited the iniquity (ungodly desire) of his father (Ex. 20:5–6). Without deliverance by Truth this person is in bondage, unreality, deception, negativity, foolishness, sickness, and evil, and he doesn't even know it....
>
> In deliverance we are released from the spirits and desires that twist our heart and deceive our mind. What is a "spirit"? Anger is a spirit. Irritation and self-pity are spirits. Hatred, jealousy, illness, worry, deception,

arrogance, fear, rebellion, resentment, phobia, shyness,
conceit, confusion, smugness, sadness, accusation,
addiction, pride, cruelty, legalism, homosexuality, reli-
giosity, complaining, lying are all names of spirits.

Every word in the dictionary that describes any kind
of evil, wicked intent, or sin against God is the name of a
demon or evil spirit.... If at any time in your life you have
ever expressed any such spirit or desire, then you still have
it hidden inside, unless you have been delivered of it.[11]

An appendix in the book contains:

a list of 1700 desires that are evil in the sight of God.
Those who have such desires will not inherit the kingdom of God.... Each word on this list represents an
iniquity as well as an evil spirit.... This list of 1700 was
edited from a list of 7600 that was itself incomplete.[12]

What does the list include? Everything ranging from acne,
arthritis, and fever to laziness, brashness, and worldliness. According
to this evangelistic ministry, a person experiences deliverance by
binding and casting out a spirit or demon. To do that people are
told to say this prayer:

I bind and rebuke you spirit of _____
In the name and blood of Jesus
And I command you to leave me now
totally and wholly....
Thank you Jesus.[13]

Along with the prayer, the ministry provided these instructions:

Speak directly to the spirit. Then cough and blow it
out. Coughing is often necessary to release the spirit....
Cough as necessary until it is out. If the spirit manifests
disruptively or violently, it may be commanded....

> Do not allow the demon to speak and alter the
> words of this prayer. If it is altered ... the demon does
> not have to obey and the demon knows this.[14]

Such methods are patently unbiblical. You'll find nothing like it in Scripture.

Paul had a great love for God's Word and wanted to obey it more than anything else, but even he occasionally struggled with indwelling sin:

> I know that nothing good dwells in me, that is, in my
> flesh; for the willing is present in me, but the doing of
> the good is not. For the good that I want, I do not
> do, but I practice the very evil that I do not want. But
> if I am doing the very thing I do not want, I am no
> longer the one doing it, but sin which dwells in me.
>
> I find then the principle that evil is present in me,
> the one who wants to do good. For I joyfully concur
> with the law of God in the inner man, but I see a dif-
> ferent law in the members of my body, waging war
> against the law of my mind and making me a prisoner
> of the law of sin which is in my members. Wretched
> man that I am! Who will set me free from the body of
> this death? (Rom. 7:18–24)

The problem was not demonic. Paul's struggle was with the flesh. Every Christian faces the same battle. But there is no incantation or abracadabra that can free us from it. Paul expressed his desire to be rid of sin and was confident of ultimate triumph over it through Jesus Christ in glory (v. 25).

Until that time, what are believers to do? Paul said, "Be strong" (1 Cor. 16:13). The Corinthians especially needed that command because they were spiritually weak. They allowed their flesh to rule. Whatever the flesh told them to do, they did it.

The command literally means "be strengthened." Now you can't strengthen yourself; that's something God has to do. In

Ephesians 3:16 Paul said we are "strengthened with power through His Spirit in the inner man." As you yield your life to the Spirit of God, you will be strengthened by His strength.

Although the Corinthians were spiritually weak, they were under the delusion that they were strong. That's why Paul rebuked them: "Who regards you as superior? What do you have that you did not receive? And if you did receive it, why do you boast as if you had not received it?" (1 Cor. 4:7). He was saying, "What makes you think you're so great? If you're different from others, it's because God made you that way. If you have anything, it's because God gave it to you."

God provides spiritual strength as we exert discipline and self-control rather than yielding to the world, the flesh, and the Devil. That's why Paul likened the Christian life to the rigorous discipline of an athlete:

> Do you not know that those who run in a race all run,
> but only one receives the prize? Run in such a way that
> you may win. Everyone who competes in the games exer-
> cises self-control in all things. They then do it to receive a
> perishable wreath, but we an imperishable. Therefore I
> run in such a way, as not without aim; I box in such a
> way, as not beating the air; but I discipline my body and
> make it my slave, so that, after I have preached to others,
> I myself will not be disqualified. (9:24–27)

The Greeks held two great athletic festivals: the Olympic games and the Isthmian games. The Isthmian games were held at Corinth. Contestants in the games had to undergo strict training for ten months. The last month was spent at Corinth, with supervised daily workouts in the gymnasium and athletic fields. Such discipline was necessary for victory.

In the spiritual realm no Christian will be spiritually successful without discipline. If an athlete expects to excel, he or she carefully supervises such things as diet, sleep, and exercise. Similarly, the believer is to follow the training rules of God's Word. He or she is not to engage in battle with a halfhearted, out-of-shape effort. His or her mind must be disciplined according to the standard of God's revealed truth.

Notice that spiritual strength has nothing to do with pulling down strongholds and commanding the forces of darkness. Paul didn't tell the Corinthians to speak directly to demons and say, "I bind and rebuke you." He didn't tell them to blow out, cough, or otherwise cajole demons to leave.

The problem is that some believers are unwilling to pay the price of discipline. Instead of yielding to the Holy Spirit, they give way to the world, the flesh, and the Devil. By doing so they hinder their spiritual growth and effectiveness in serving the Lord. Then they look for a quick fix—a canned prayer, a magic phrase, or a holy cough.

What about you? Are you allowing the Lord to strengthen you? Is your life marked by discipline and self-control? Do you regularly study God's Word, pray, and have fellowship with other believers? Are you obeying the divine training rules of God's Word? Are you willing to pay the price of living for the Lord?

BE LOVING

Picture yourself suited up and ready for battle. You've just received four apostolic commands for marching orders. Now Paul said, "Let all that you do be done in love" (1 Cor. 16:14). That final command balances unretreating courage with unfailing love. Both need to exist side by side for either one to be effective. If you have too much love and not enough doctrine, you will be washed away by sentimentalism. If you have too much doctrine and not enough love, you'll develop a harsh attitude.

The Corinthians were not conducting themselves with an attitude of love. They were fighting with each other, acting immorally, suing each other, causing weaker believers to stumble, and being disrespectful at the Lord's Table. That's why Paul called them to sound doctrine and love.

What is your responsibility in spiritual warfare? Strap on the armor with prayer. Be alert, firm, mature, strong, and loving. Those are scriptural commands for victorious living. If you make them your strongholds, you will *win* the battle!

READERS' GUIDE

Before beginning your personal or group study of *Standing Strong*, take time to read these introductory comments.

If you are working through the study on your own, you may want to adapt certain sections (for example, the icebreakers), and record your responses to all questions in a separate notebook. You might find it more enriching or motivating to study with a partner with whom you can share answers or insights.

If you are leading a group, you may want to ask your group members to read each assigned chapter and work through the study questions before the group meets. This isn't always easy for busy adults, so encourage them with occasional phone calls or notes between meetings. Help members manage their time by pointing out how they can cover a few pages each day. Also have them identify a regular time of the day or week that they can devote to the study. They too may write their responses to the questions in notebooks.

Notice that each session includes the following features:

> **Chapter Theme**—a brief statement summarizing the
> chapter.
>
> **Icebreaker**—an activity to help group members get bet-
> ter acquainted with the session topic and/or with
> each other.
>
> **Group Discovery Questions**—a list of questions to
> encourage individual discovery or group participation.

Personal Application Questions—an aid to applying the
knowledge gained through study to one's personal living. (Note: These are important questions for group
members to answer for themselves, even if they do not
wish to discuss their responses in the meeting.)

Focus on Prayer—suggestions for turning one's learning
into prayer.

Assignment—activities or preparation to complete prior
to the next session.

Here are a few tips that can help you more effectively lead small-group
studies:

Pray for each group member, asking the Lord to help you
create an open atmosphere where everyone will feel
free to share with one another and you.

Encourage group members to bring their Bibles as well as
their texts to each session. This study is based on the
New International Version, but it is good to have several translations on hand for purposes of comparison.

Start and end on time. This is especially important for
the first meeting because it will set the pattern for the
rest of the sessions.

Begin with prayer, asking the Holy Spirit to open hearts
and minds and to give understanding so that truth
will be applied.

Involve everyone. As learners, we retain only 10% of what
we hear; 20% of what we see; 65% of what we hear
and see; but 90% of what we hear, see, and do.

Promote a relaxed environment. Arrange the chairs in a
circle or semicircle. This allows eye contact among
members and encourages dynamic discussion. Be
relaxed in your own attitude and manner. Be willing
to share yourself.

CHAPTER 1
DRAWING THE BATTLE LINES

Chapter Theme: As believers, we play a key role in the ongoing cosmic conflict between God and Satan.

ICEBREAKERS (CHOOSE ONE)

1. When someone is in conflict with another person, what usually initiates the conflict? How does the interpersonal conflict manifest itself?
2. Suppose you are an employer. How would you feel if your most beloved and trusted worker suddenly turned against you and tried to sabotage your business, with the ultimate goal of supplanting you?

GROUP DISCOVERY QUESTIONS

1. What lofty position did God give to Lucifer?
2. What was Satan proud of? What did it produce? How did it manifest itself?
3. How widespread is Satan's army? In what ways do you see its effects in the world today?
4. Why is Christ Satan's primary target?
5. Explain the purpose God had in sending the archangel Michael to help another holy angel defeat Satan's emissary. With that in mind, can you give some contemporary examples of nations that have opposed God's purposes in the past but don't do so now?
6. In what ways do you see Satan attacking Israel today?

PERSONAL APPLICATION QUESTIONS

1. Satan's pride was the beginning of his fall, which extended to all humanity. How does the sin of pride spawn other sins?
2. How does the conflict between God and Satan express itself in your life? Contrast the spiritual fruit Christ produces with the fleshly fruit Satan encourages. What kind of fruit are you manifesting?
3. What can you learn from the example of Daniel's ongoing prayers to God on behalf of his people? What should you be praying for in regard to the outworking of God's plans in the world?

FOCUS ON PRAYER

Ask God to give you a better understanding of how His conflict with Satan manifests itself in the world. Ask Him also to strengthen you to resist the temptations Satan brings into your life.

ASSIGNMENTS

1. Read chapter 2 of the text and answer the corresponding questions.
2. Read 1 Timothy 2:1–2. List some specific prayer requests for world leaders, reflecting on their role in global spiritual warfare.

CHAPTER 2
SATAN AS GOD'S INSTRUMENT

Chapter Theme: God uses even Satan and his demons to accomplish His sovereign will for believers and unbelievers alike.

ICEBREAKERS (CHOOSE ONE)

1. What do you suppose motivates an athlete to train for endless hours to compete in his or her chosen sport? How might that relate to any Christian faced with trials or afflictions?
2. If you have children, what things do they do that require you to discipline them? Relate some specific examples.

GROUP DISCOVERY QUESTIONS

1. How have people in today's spiritual-warfare movement concluded that it is possible for a demon to indwell a believer? What is wrong with their reasoning?
2. Why did God allow Satan to afflict Job? What did Job learn from his afflictions?
3. In what ways did God use the afflictions experienced by both Paul and Peter to strengthen their faith?
4. Why did God allow a demon to torment Saul? What must happen before Satan and his demons can terrorize anyone?
5. Why was Paul so adamant that the Corinthian church deliver an unrepentant sinner in their midst to Satan? Why should church discipline never be neglected?

6. Describe how today's spiritual-warfare movement can become a detriment to what God wants to accomplish.

PERSONAL APPLICATION QUESTIONS

1. Job's test is great proof of God's sovereignty in every aspect of our lives. The next time you face a difficult trial and you don't understand what God is doing, reflect on what you have learned about Job and how it can be a source of comfort to you.
2. In what specific ways do you see God's love manifested in your life? Read again what Samuel Bolton said. What additional things can you add to the ways you see God's love for you?

FOCUS ON PRAYER

Ask God to give you a greater sensitivity to His sovereign control over your life. Ask Him to reveal to you the reality of Romans 8:28.

ASSIGNMENTS

1. Read chapter 3 of the text and answer the questions in the corresponding study.
2. For the next few days, make note of each obstacle that comes your way. What was your initial reaction? After your list has several items on it, look at those obstacles in the light of God's sovereign plan for your life.

CHAPTER 3
SATAN ATTACKS THE CHURCH

Chapter Theme: God allows Satan to attack His church—in some cases as a judgment on sin and in others as a means of strengthening faith and commitment.

ICEBREAKERS (CHOOSE ONE)

1. Christ warned five of the churches about something they were doing that displeased Him. Name some of the things prevalent in Christianity today that you think displease God.
2. How do you usually respond when God gives you an opportunity to be a witness for Christ?

GROUP DISCOVERY QUESTIONS

1. Contrast what the Bible says about our security from demons with what is being taught about "territorial warfare."
2. What one thing had the church at Ephesus failed in? What usually results from that?
3. What was the basic problem with the church at Pergamum? What motivated them to do what they did?
4. How did Christ encourage those who did not follow the deep things of Satan in the church at Thyatira? Why is it essential for the church to draw the line between right and wrong?
5. What are the benefits of true repentance? How does that relate to God's battle plan for spiritual warfare?
6. Give some examples of churches today that fit the model of the church at Laodicea. What does Christ want those types of churches to do?
7. What preservative characterized the church at Philadelphia? Why is that preservative so effective?
8. How did God preserve the church at Smyrna? Why does that preservative work?

PERSONAL APPLICATION QUESTIONS

1. Are you in danger of losing your first love—or maybe have you lost it already? Think back to when you first embraced Christ—when your new life in Him was rich and exciting and you experienced the thrill of being free from the bondage of sin. Have other things replaced that zeal in your life? If so, you need to repent and ask God to forgive your indifference toward Him.
2. Living in today's materialistic world is a great temptation to many believers. In what ways does the world assault you, drawing you away from loving service to Christ? What is your best defense against the world's temptations?
3. God uses both evangelism and persecution to preserve His church in this world. What must you do for God to make them real in your life? What will happen when you take advantage of the opportunities God gives you for evangelism? When are you most likely to be persecuted for your faith? Are you willing to pay the price?

FOCUS ON PRAYER

Ask God to give you a greater love for Him as a result of your willingness to stand separate from the world. Pray that He would give you opportunities to present the claims of Christ.

ASSIGNMENTS

1. Read chapter 4 of the text and answer the questions in the corresponding study.
2. Take notice of the doors God opens for you this week to minister to unbelievers. It may not even be an opportunity to share the gospel right away, but a chance to establish a relationship that could easily lead to that opportunity.

CHAPTER 4
THE BELIEVER'S DUTY

Chapter Theme: We grow in Christ when we are obedient to Him, which includes our commitment to endure hardship, fight the good fight, and stand firm in the battle.

ICEBREAKERS (CHOOSE ONE)

1. The apostle Paul likened the Christian to a soldier. How would you characterize a soldier's duty?
2. What things in the world most often prevent you from fulfilling what God expects from you?

GROUP DISCOVERY QUESTIONS

1. What must a Christian be doing before he or she could be characterized as a good soldier who endures hardship?
2. How can we take encouragement from Christ's life when we are faced with adversity?
3. Explain how the prosperity gospel contradicts the biblical meaning of discipleship.
4. How does Scripture tell us to resist Satan? What does that require us to know?
5. What kind of warfare are we engaged in? How would you characterize the weapons God has given us for this warfare?

6. Explain the quietist and pietist views of the Christian life. What is wrong
   with each extreme?

PERSONAL APPLICATION QUESTIONS

1. In Luke 9, Christ offered three people the opportunity to follow Him,
   but they all had something that kept them from making a full commitment. What about you? Examine yourself to see what worldly things
   might be keeping you from following Christ wholeheartedly.
2. How does our contemporary Christian experience differ from what Paul
   experienced? What must happen in your life before you could fit the
   description offered by J. C. Ryle?
3. Read Matthew 4:1–11. How did Jesus resist the Devil? What can you
   learn from Christ's example whenever you are tempted to sin?

FOCUS ON PRAYER

Ask God to give you a greater awareness of the spiritual battle that is taking place daily. Ask Him to help you apply your scriptural knowledge to every
occasion when you are tempted to sin.

ASSIGNMENTS

1. Read chapter 5 of the text and answer the questions in the corresponding study.
2. Reexamine the list of the Christian armor. Next to each, indicate why
   you think God provides that piece of armor.

CHAPTER 5
THE CALL TO COMMITMENT

Chapter Theme: God calls all Christians to don the belt of truthfulness,
which is being committed and ready for the battle.

ICEBREAKERS (CHOOSE ONE)

1. Before you leave your home to go to work, to school, or on some
   errand, what do you need to do? Why?
2. Describe the transformation that occurs when a caterpillar changes into a
   butterfly. What does it leave behind?

GROUP DISCOVERY QUESTIONS

1. How does Satan attempt to get you to doubt God? How should you respond?
2. Why is it difficult to live the Christian life in contemporary Western culture?
3. In what ways does putting on the belt of truthfulness prepare the Christian for battle?
4. What part does self-sacrifice play in being committed to Christ? What must be transformed before that can happen?
5. What does the pursuit of excellence require?

PERSONAL APPLICATION QUESTIONS

1. Cite some examples of times you doubted God. What caused you to doubt Him? What kinds of difficulties do you often face that hinder your relationship with Christ? Once you identify those causes, seek to either avoid or be ready for them in the future.
2. Analyze your commitment level to Christ and His cause. How does it relate to the zeal of the young man who joined the Israeli Army so he could be in the most difficult regiment? To be honest, can you relate more with those who serve only when it's convenient—when it fits with their agenda? Read Romans 12:1–2 and be sure you are living like one who has decided to follow Jesus.
3. Are you guilty of masking your problems or your struggles with sin from other believers? Don't allow Satan such a hold on you; share your struggles with a close Christian friend and let God use him or her to encourage and advise you.

FOCUS ON PRAYER

Ask God to help you be prepared for the battle by showing you how to renew your mind. Ask Him to reveal to you any areas in your life that you need to yield more completely to His control.

ASSIGNMENTS

1. Read chapter 6 of the text and answer the questions in the corresponding study.
2. Make a list of all the commitments you have, such as your job, responsibilities at church or a Bible study, and so on. Which ones are related to tasks? Which ones are related to people? Which ones involve service to Christ?

CHAPTER 6
PROTECTING OUR MINDS AND EMOTIONS

Chapter Theme: To protect your mind and emotions from Satan's relentless attack, you must be clothed with the breastplate of righteousness.

ICEBREAKERS (CHOOSE ONE)

1. In what ways do you entertain yourself? What are the things you desire most in life?
2. In what specific ways do you experience conflict because of your Christianity?

GROUP DISCOVERY QUESTIONS

1. What does Satan attempt to do to believers when he attacks their will and emotions?
2. In what ways do the proponents of today's spiritual-warfare movement err in following the example of Christ and His apostles?
3. Why can't the breastplate of righteousness refer to our own righteousness?
4. What happens to an individual the moment he or she is saved? Why is that necessary?
5. What kind of effort is required to live a holy life?

PERSONAL APPLICATION QUESTIONS

1. In what ways is Satan most successful in attacking your mind and emotions? In what ways are you most influenced by the world? How can a commitment to practicing the righteousness of Christ enable you to resist Satan's attacks?
2. What is your attitude toward repentance? Do you acknowledge your sin to God, but not really work at eliminating it from your life? If so, you haven't truly repented. Determine to make your repentance real by forsaking sin.

FOCUS ON PRAYER

Ask God to reveal to you the sins you hide and don't deal with. Commit Psalm 139:23–24 to memory and let that be your prayer.

ASSIGNMENTS

1. Read chapter 7 of the text and answer the questions in the corresponding study.
2. For the next week, note each time you find yourself agreeing with or being influenced by something that reflects the world's thinking. Line those things up against God's Word. Which ones must you discard? Get in the habit of taking every thought captive to the obedience of Christ.

CHAPTER 7
THE GOOD NEWS OF PEACE

Chapter Theme: Without the confidence we gain from knowing we are at peace with God, we would not be able to stand firm in the midst of our battle with Satan.

ICEBREAKERS (CHOOSE ONE)

1. How do you feel when you are by yourself and you have to confront someone or be confronted by someone? How different did you feel on similar occasions when a friend accompanied you?
2. Think of the last time you were faced with a situation where God's Word clearly indicated that you should do a certain thing that you didn't want to do. What happened if you obeyed? What happened if you didn't?

GROUP DISCOVERY QUESTIONS

1. Why is it important to understand that Ephesians 6:15 doesn't refer to preaching the gospel?
2. Describe the war between God and humanity. Why does everyone start out as an enemy of God?
3. How did God make peace with you? How does He maintain it?
4. What must you do with any teaching or experience another Christian claims to have had?
5. What enables the Christian to stand with confidence in the midst of the spiritual battle?

PERSONAL APPLICATION QUESTIONS

1. How would you respond if someone attacked the reality of your Christianity, pointing out that you are much less than perfect? What truth would you share with him or her regarding the peace that you have with God? What could you share about Christ that would explain the remedy He provided for your sin?
2. Since Christ your High Priest is continually interceding before God on your behalf, what does that require from you? Since you no longer are an enemy but a son or daughter, what ought to characterize your relationship to God?

FOCUS ON PRAYER

Thank God for making peace with you through the sacrifice of Christ. Thank Him for Christ's intercession before God on your behalf.

ASSIGNMENTS

1. Read chapter 8 of the text and answer the questions in the corresponding study.
2. Plan out what you might tell an unbeliever about the peace that God offers in Christ. Use some of the truths in this chapter and add other facts that would reinforce the fact that God is at war with those who don't know Him.

CHAPTER 8
FAITH: OUR DEFENSE SHIELD

Chapter Theme: The best way we can defend ourselves against the fiery darts of Satan's temptations is by raising the shield of our faith in God.

ICEBREAKERS (CHOOSE ONE)

1. What are the benefits of exercise? How does exercise affect your ability to do certain activities?
2. What usually happens when you go through a trial? How does that trial affect your relationship with God?

GROUP DISCOVERY QUESTIONS

1. What distinctions did Paul make among the individual pieces of armor? Why?
2. Define faith. Why is faith necessary before we can resist Satan's attacks?
3. Explain how exercising our faith is a matter of obedience.
4. What happens when our faith is tested by trials?
5. Describe how Satan tempted Christ in the wilderness. What methods does he use to tempt us?
6. What is the only way to defend ourselves against Satan's temptations? What does that require of you?

PERSONAL APPLICATION QUESTIONS

1. Read Hebrews 11. What lessons can you learn from these heroes of faith that you can apply to your life?
2. In what ways do you experience temptation today? How do you plan to use the shield of faith to defend yourself against each of those temptations?

FOCUS ON PRAYER

Ask God to strengthen your faith by helping you gain a more heavenly perspective throughout each day. Ask Him to help you apply His Word to those events that tend to pull you away from dependence on Him.

ASSIGNMENTS

1. Read chapter 9 of the text and answer the questions in the corresponding study.
2. During the time you normally have your devotions, start this habit: Whenever you come across a command that particularly applies to you, write it down. Refer to it often as you make obedience to that command a reflexive act in your daily walk.

CHAPTER 9
THE BELIEVER'S FUTURE GLORY

Chapter Theme: Satan's two major methods of attack are discouragement and doubt. But by putting on the helmet of the hope of salvation, you can resist his attacks.

ICEBREAKERS (CHOOSE ONE)

1. What is the goal of most athletes when they run a race? How effective
   do you think their training would be if once they started the race, they
   had no goal?
2. Have you ever had to guard something for someone? What were you
   responsible to do? Could there have been some reason for ceasing to
   guard that thing?

GROUP DISCOVERY QUESTIONS

1. What are the three aspects of salvation? Explain their significance in
   your life.
2. What are the ramifications of knowing that your future glorification is
   secure in Christ?
3. How does Satan attempt to discourage believers?
4. What does Satan try to get believers to doubt? Why?
5. Identify seven strands that assure us that Christ holds on to us eternally.
6. What guarantee did God give to assure us of the reality of our salvation?
   How does that guarantee work?
7. What keeps us secure from Satan's attacks?

PERSONAL APPLICATION QUESTIONS

1. To what degree do you exult in your tribulations? How often do you
   focus on the trial and not on the benefits? According to Romans 5:2–5,
   what are the benefits of our tribulations? How can you turn the results
   of tribulation into goals for your life?
2. In what ways are you most often discouraged? How often are you plagued
   with doubts about your salvation? How do you think the helmet of the
   hope of salvation can help you turn discouraging things into positive
   events and turn your doubt into complete trust in God?

FOCUS ON PRAYER

Ask God to give you a better appreciation of the salvation He has given
you. Thank Him for providing such a secure salvation—one in which simply
looking to what you will have in heaven makes life that much better on earth.

ASSIGNMENTS

1. Read chapter 10 of the text and answer the questions in the corresponding study.
2. Read Romans 8. Make note of each phrase that indicates how the Holy Spirit guarantees the security of your salvation. Write down each of those guarantees. The next time you are faced with any discouragement or doubt, refer back to your notes.

CHAPTER 10
THE SWORD OF THE SPIRIT

Chapter Theme: Perhaps the most versatile weapon available to you as a Christian is the sword of the Spirit. With it you can parry Satan's attack and also cut through Satan's dominion to bring the truth to lost souls.

ICEBREAKERS (CHOOSE ONE)

1. Why do you need a map when you drive into an unknown area? Why do you need a guidebook when you go to a museum? Why do you need a set of instructions when you buy an appliance?
2. When you have been able to share the gospel with people, telling them what Christ did on their behalf, what kind of reactions did you receive? Describe them.

GROUP DISCOVERY QUESTIONS

1. Since God's Word is authoritative, how should Christians respond to it? Why?
2. In what ways is God's Word sufficient?
3. Why is it critical to use God's Word in a defensive manner? Since believers cannot bind Satan, what should they do?
4. What does Christ's response to three of Satan's temptations teach us about applying God's Word?
5. Are signs and wonders necessary for evangelism? Why or why not?
6. How does Satan counterattack the believer's use of the sword in evangelism?

PERSONAL APPLICATION QUESTIONS

1. Review the section that details the divine qualities of God's Word. In what ways can those qualities encourage you to take God's Word more seriously?

2. Since God's Word is defensive, you can use it to fend off Satan's attacks. What specific temptations do you struggle with most? Seek out what God's Word teaches about those temptations so that the next time you are tempted, you'll be ready to resist.

3. Are you a sower of God's Word? Do you talk about the good news of Christ with the lost as God gives you opportunity, or do you shy away? Notice that in Matthew 13:3–8 the sower does not discriminate where he sows—he is not responsible for casting seed on good ground—his only responsibility is to sow the seed. Where do you need to start sowing seed?

FOCUS ON PRAYER

Ask God to help you be ready and willing to make a defense of the hope that is in you (1 Peter 3:15). Ask Him particularly to help you recall what His Word teaches about specific struggles you have.

ASSIGNMENTS

1. Read chapter 11 of the text and answer the questions in the corresponding study.

2. Review the story about the butterfly, botanist, and bee. Which one most closely resembles your personal Bible study habits? Starting today, begin to read and study the Bible with the attitude of the bee. Study especially with the purpose of obeying God's Word by applying what it teaches. Don't let a day go by where you have not mined some nugget of truth from God's rich resource.

CHAPTER 11
PRAYERS ON THE BATTLEGROUND

Chapter Theme: While we must be prepared for battle by wearing the spiritual armor God has provided, we must have a commitment to unceasing prayer for the armor to be effective.

ICEBREAKERS (CHOOSE ONE)

1. Which of the following words best describes your prayer life: intense, intimate, lackadaisical, sporadic, incredible, joyful, quiet, nonexistent, frequent? Why?

2. Modern warfare depends heavily on communication. During the Gulf War, what line of Iraqi defense did U.S. forces attempt to destroy first? What was the result? What do you suppose Satan tries to eliminate first in spiritual warfare?

GROUP DISCOVERY QUESTIONS

1. Why are so-called warfare prayers ineffective in dealing with Satan?
2. Why is prayer important in conjunction with spiritual armor? What may result from a lack of prayer?
3. What does it mean to pray at all times? What are you saying to God through your lack of prayer?
4. How does the Holy Spirit help us pray?
5. In Christ's hour of temptation in the garden of Gethsemane, how did He overcome Satan's efforts? What did Christ teach the disciples about prayer?
6. Who are we to pray for? How can we know what they need prayer for?

PERSONAL APPLICATION QUESTIONS

1. How often do you pray? How do you pray? When you pray, how much time do you spend? Learn to cultivate an attitude of prayer throughout the day. Begin to meditate on God's Word as you study it each day. Allow God's Spirit to develop in you a spiritual sensitivity to the things that happen around you. Try to see those things as God sees them.
2. Prayer is hard work, as you well know. How often have you had great intentions to spend time in prayer but like the disciples in the garden of Gethsemane let down your guard? When are you most susceptible to neglect prayer? When or in what circumstances do you find yourself the most successful in persevering? As you begin to isolate what prevents you from praying and simply remember that God has commanded you to pray at all times, you'll begin to see your resistance to temptation and your perseverance increase.

FOCUS ON PRAYER

Ask God to reveal Himself in greater measure to you as you meditate on His character. Also ask Him to reveal to you your own sin and self-sufficiency—the very things that most often keep you from communing with Him.

ASSIGNMENTS

1. Read chapter 12 of the text and answer the questions in the corresponding study.
2. Pick your favorite prayer in the Bible and study it. What was the individual praying for? Why? What can you learn from that prayer and apply to your own prayer life?

CHAPTER 12
THE COMMANDS FOR VICTORY

Chapter Theme: Our success in spiritual warfare is based on five commands that the apostle Paul issued in 1 Corinthians 16: being alert, firm, mature, strong, and loving.

ICEBREAKERS (CHOOSE ONE)

1. What kinds of activities do you participate in that require you to be alert? What are the potential dangers of not being in that state of mind?
2. In what areas of your life do you habitually exercise self-discipline? Why? What might happen if you didn't?

GROUP DISCOVERY QUESTIONS

1. How can you best defend yourself against Satan's surprise attacks?
2. What kinds of attacks should you be prepared for?
3. What are three possible explanations for those who claim to have cast out demons and performed signs and wonders?
4. What is the best way to protect yourself from the influence of false teachers?
5. How can you "stand firm in the faith"?
6. What must ultimately verify the authenticity of your experiences?
7. What must believers do to become mature? Why do so many remain immature?
8. How can you obey God's command to be strong?

PERSONAL APPLICATION QUESTIONS

1. In the commands to be alert, firm, and mature, what is the key ingredient you must turn to before you can obey those commands? How much time and commitment are you willing to devote in doing that?

2. If an athlete must watch over his dietary, rest, and exercise habits to be successful in competition, what are the types of things you need to watch over to be successful in the spiritual realm? Take a close look at how disciplined you are in dealing with sin and committing yourself to prayer, Bible study, and fellowship with other believers. In which areas do you need to exercise more self-discipline?

FOCUS ON PRAYER

Ask God to help you become more obedient to Him by gaining a greater appreciation of the spiritual battle raging about you. Ask Him to give you a greater devotion to His Word and a greater willingness to yield your life to the control of His Spirit.

ASSIGNMENT

Review the assignments you have been asked to do for the previous chapters. In what ways have you found them beneficial to your walk with Christ? If there are assignments you still need to complete, please do so. Don't forget the principles you have learned in the preceding pages—make sure they remain a part of your ongoing commitment to become more like Christ.

Notes

ᴄᴗ

Introduction

1. C. S. Lewis, *The Screwtape Letters* (New York: Macmillan, 1961), 3.
2. John Dart, "Evangelicals, Charismatics Prepare for Spiritual Warfare," *Los Angeles Times*, February 17, 1990, F16.
3. Archibald Alexander, *Thoughts on Religious Experience* (Carlisle, PA: The Banner of Truth Trust, 1978), xviii.

Chapter 1

1. *Los Angeles Times,* November 20, 1991, A23.

Chapter 2

1. C. Fred Dickason, *Angels Elect and Evil* (Chicago: Moody Press, 1975), 191.
2. C. Fred Dickason, *Demon Possession & the Christian* Westchester, IL: Crossway, 1987), 40.
3. Ibid., 127.
4. Ibid., 157.
5. Ibid., 273.

6. Merrill Unger, *What Demons Can Do to Saints* (Chicago: Moody Press, 1977), 51–52.
7. Jonathan Edwards, *The Experience That Counts!* edited by N. R. Needham (London: Grace Publications Trust, 1991), 89–90.
8. Charles Hodge, *Commentary on the Epistle to the Romans* (Grand Rapids: Eerdmans, 1972), 395.
9. Edwards, *Experience*, 99.
10. J. I. Packer, *Knowing God* (Downers Grove, IL: InterVarsity, 1973), 227.
11. Gleason Archer, *The Book of Job* (Grand Rapids: Baker, 1982), 18.
12. Jerry Bridges, *Trusting God* (Colorado Springs: NavPress, 1988), 122.
13. R. C. H. Lenski, *The Interpretation of St. Luke's Gospel* (Minneapolis: Augsburg, 1961), 1034.
14. Homer Kent, *The Pastoral Epistles* (Chicago: Moody Press, 1986), 94.
15. Samuel Bolton, *The Bounds of Christian Freedom* (Edinburgh: The Banner of Truth Trust, 1964), 25.

CHAPTER 3

1. Timothy Warner, *Engaging the Enemy: How to Fight and Defeat Territorial Demons,* edited by C. Peter Wagner (Ventura, CA: Regal, 1991), 52.
2. Steven Lawson, "Defeating Territorial Spirits," *Charisma and the Christian Life,* April 1990, 48.
3. C. Peter Wagner, "Territorial Spirits and World Mission," *Evangelical Missions Quarterly,* July 1989, 286.
4. John Dawson, "Winning the Battle for Your Neighborhood," *Charisma and the Christian Life,* April 1990, 60–61.
5. Cited in Win Worley, *Battling the Hosts of Hell: Diary of an Exorcist* (Lansing, IL: H.B.C., 1980), 195.
6. Sinclair Ferguson, "The Fear of the Lord: Seeing God as He Is," *Discipleship Journal* 52 (1989): 42.
7. H. B. Workman, *Persecution in the Early Church* (Cincinnati: Jennings and Graham, n.d.), 103–4.

CHAPTER 4

1. Mark I. Bubeck, *The Adversary: The Christian versus Demon Activity* (Chicago: Moody Press, 1975), 78.
2. Ken L. Sarles, "A Theological Evaluation of the Prosperity Gospel," *Bibliotheca Sacra* 143 (October–December 1986): 336, 344–45.
3. For more information see my book *Charismatic Chaos* (Grand Rapids: Zondervan, 1992), chapter 12.
4. William Hendriksen, *Exposition of Thessalonians, Timothy and Titus* (Grand Rapids: Baker, 1957), 315.
5. J. C. Ryle, *Holiness* (Hertfordshire, England: Evangelical Press, 1989), 62.

6. Martyn Lloyd-Jones, *The Christian Soldier* (Grand Rapids: Baker, 1977), 179.
7. For further discussion on this issue see my book *Our Sufficiency in Christ* (Dallas: Word, 1991), chapter 12.

CHAPTER 5

1. Theodore Roosevelt (speech, Hamilton Club, Chicago, April 10, 1899).
2. Peter Masters, *The Healing Epidemic* (London: The Wakeman Trust, 1988), 92.
3. Mark I. Bubeck, *The Satanic Revival* (San Bernardino, CA: Here's Life, 1991), 11.
4. Saint Augustine, *The City of God* (Garden City, NY: Image Books, 1958), 14:28.
5. Neil Anderson, *The Bondage Breaker* (Eugene, OR: Harvest House, 1990), 149–51.
6. Ibid., chapter 4.
7. Charles Spurgeon, *The Soul-Winner* (New York: Revell, 1895), 28–29.
8. Thomas Watson, *A Body of Divinity* (Carlisle, PA: The Banner of Truth Trust, 1986), 241, 247.
9. James Montgomery Boice, *Philippians: An Expositional Commentary* (Grand Rapids: Zondervan, 1971), 55.

CHAPTER 6

1. John Bunyan, *The Holy War* (Springdale, PA: Whitaker House, 1985), 5–9.
2. Timothy Warner, *Spiritual Warfare* (Wheaton, IL: Crossway, 1991), 19.
3. C. Peter Wagner, *How to Have a Healing Ministry* (Ventura, CA: Regal, 1988), 257.

4. Masters, *Healing Epidemic*, 62, 82–83.
5. J. C. Ryle, *Holiness* (Welwyn, England: Evangelical Press, 1979), 555.
6. *Webster's Ninth New Collegiate Dictionary.*
7. William Gurnall, *The Christian in Complete Armour* (Carlisle, PA: The Banner of Truth Trust, 1967), 1; 453.

CHAPTER 7

1. Masters, *Healing Epidemic*, 15–16.

CHAPTER 8

1. Ben Patterson, "Cause for Concern," *Christianity Today*, August 8, 1986, 20.
2. See John MacArthur, *Charismatic Chaos* (Grand Rapids: Zondervan, 1992), chapter 6.
3. Dick Bernal, *Engaging the Enemy: How to Fight and Defeat Territorial Spirits*, edited by C. Peter Wagner (Ventura, CA: Regal), 98, 107.
4. Martyn Lloyd-Jones, *Spiritual Depression* (Grand Rapids: Eerdmans, 1965), 227–28.
5. Cited in Harold Ivan Smith, "Sex and Singleness the Second Time Around," *Christianity Today*, May 25, 1979, 18.

CHAPTER 9

1. Peter H. Davids, *Wrestling with Dark Angels*, edited by C. Peter Wagner and F. Douglas Pennoyer (Ventura, CA: Regal, 1990), 220, 233.
2. J. I. Packer, "Poor Health May Be the Best Remedy," *Christianity Today*, May 21, 1982, 15.

3. Joni Eareckson Tada, *A Step Further* (Grand Rapids: Zondervan, 1978), 136, 140–41, 155.
4. John Murray, *The Epistle to the Romans* (Grand Rapids: Eerdmans, 1965), 165.
5. Leon Morris, *The Gospel According to John* (Grand Rapids: Eerdmans, 1971), 521.
6. Dickason, *Demon Possession*, 162.
7. Ibid., 163.
8. Ibid.
9. Frederick S. Leahy, *Satan Cast Out* (Carlisle, PA: The Banner of Truth Trust, 1975), 96.

CHAPTER 10

1. Vera Kadaeva, "Taking the Gospel to the Barricades," *Grace Today*, November 24, 1991, 1–4.
2. Dickason, *Demon Possession*, 199–205.
3. John MacArthur, *The MacArthur New Testament Commentary: Matthew 16–23* (Chicago: Moody Press, 1988), 33–34.
4. John Wimber and Kevin Springer, *Power Evangelism* (San Francisco: Harper & Row, 1986), emphasis added by the author.
5. John Wimber, quoted in C. Peter Wagner and Douglas Pennoyer, eds., *Wrestling with Dark Angels* (Ventura, CA: Regal, 1990), 31.
6. Peter Masters and John Whitcomb, *The Charismatic Phenomenon* (London: The Wakeman Trust, 1982), 79.
7. Ken L. Sarles, "An Appraisal of the Signs and Wonders Movement," *Bibliotheca Sacra* 145 (January–March 1988): 80.
8. Charles Hodge, *An Exposition of the Second Epistle to the Corinthians* (Grand Rapids: Eerdmans, n.d.), 290–91.

CHAPTER 11

1. John Wimber and Kevin Springer, *Power Healing* (San Francisco: Harper & Row, 1987), 209–10.
2. Bubeck, *Adversary*, 106.
3. Ibid., 148.
4. Ibid., 150–51.
5. Richard Baxter, *The Practical Works of Richard Baxter*, (Ligonier, PA: Soli Deo Gloria, 1990), 1, 484.
6. Lloyd-Jones, *Christian Soldier*, 342.
7. Cited in Arthur Bennett, ed., *The Valley of Vision: A Collection of Puritan Prayers and Quotations* (Carlisle, PA: The Banner of Truth Trust, 1975), 181.
8. Lloyd-Jones, *Christian Soldier*, 357.
9. Ibid., 358.
10. Packer, *Knowing God*, 27.

9. Alexander, *Thoughts*, xviii.
10. Bubeck, *Satanic Revival*, 183–84.
11. Alpha-Omega Energies, *The Truth in Deliverance* (Austin, TX: Alpha-Omega Energies, n.d.), 3–4.
12. Ibid., 172.
13. Ibid., 21.
14. Ibid., 21–22.

CHAPTER 12

1. Norman Schwarzkopf, quoted in "A Mud Soldier's General Reflects on the Risks of War," *U.S. News and World Report*, February 11, 1991, 37.
2. Tom Mathews, "Remembering Pearl Harbor," *Newsweek*, November 25, 1991, 30.
3. Ibid., 38.
4. Thomas Brooks, *Precious Remedies against Satan's Devices* (Carlisle, PA: The Banner of Truth Trust, 1987), 28.
5. Thomas Ice and Robert Dean, *A Holy Rebellion* (Eugene, OR: Harvest House, 1990), 187.
6. Lewis, *Screwtape Letters*, 8.
7. Wimber and Springer, *Power Evangelism*, 88–89.
8. Sarles, "Appraisal of the Signs," *Bibliotheca Sacra*, 69–70.

Scripture Index

SUBJECT INDEX